Play Directing: The Basics introduces theatre students to a step-by-step process for directing plays, including advice on devising.

Beginning with a historical overview of directing, this book covers every aspect of the director's job from first read to closing night. Practical advice on finding plays to produce, analyzing scripts, collaborating with the design team, rehearsing with actors, devising company creations, and opening a show are peppered with advice from working professionals and academic directors. A practical workbook, short exercises, helpful websites, and suggested reading encourage readers towards a deeper study of the art of directing.

This book empowers high school and early college students interested in theatre and directing to find their own voice, develop a practice, and refine their process.

Damon Kiely is a Professor of Directing and Acting for the Theatre School of DePaul University, a professional director, and playwright.

The Basics Series

The Basics is a highly successful series of accessible guidebooks which provide an overview of the fundamental principles of a subject area in a jargon-free and undaunting format.

Intended for students approaching a subject for the first time, the books both introduce the essentials of a subject and provide an ideal springboard for further study. With over 50 titles spanning subjects from artificial intelligence (AI) to women's studies, *The Basics* are an ideal starting point for students seeking to understand a subject area.

Each text comes with recommendations for further study and gradually introduces the complexities and nuances within a subject.

PLAY DIRECTING

THE BASICS

Damon Kiely

Routledge
Taylor & Francis Group

NEW YORK AND LONDON

Cover image: Shutterstock

First published 2023
by Routledge
605 Third Avenue, New York, NY 10158

and by Routledge
4 Park Square, Milton Park, Abingdon, Oxon, OX14 4RN

Routledge is an imprint of the Taylor & Francis Group, an informa business

Library of Congress Cataloging-in-Publication Data
A catalog record for this title has been requested

ISBN: 9780367861032 (hbk)
ISBN: 9780367861049 (pbk)
ISBN: 9781003016922 (ebk)

DOI: 10.4324/9781003016922

Typeset in Bembo
by Newgen Publishing UK

To my wife, Jennifer Tanaka,
for teaching me how to write.

CONTENTS

ACKNOWLEDGMENTS

I'd like to thank my editors, Lucia Accorsi and Stacey Walker for their patience and flexibility as I pivoted to writing this book in the middle of a global pandemic. They were always supportive, clear, and gracious.

DePaul University, where I have called home for the last fifteen years, has supported my scholarship for many years: financially, with time, and with encouragement. I want to thank my many colleagues at The Theatre School of DePaul who have taught me how to be a better collaborator and teacher. Their ideas and beliefs about how to collaborate on making art are all over this book.

Generous early readers encouraged me when it was merited and gently pointed out the error of my ways. I can't thank them enough for their time and clarity of thought, especially Erin Kraft, April Cleveland, and Rachel Walshe. Student workers also contributed to the success of this book including Sam Kerns and Christine Freije.

I drew much of the wisdom for this book from the countless interviews I've had with directing colleagues throughout the world. I can't thank them enough for sharing their best insights into the craft of directing. Special thanks to friends and colleagues, Robert O'Hara, Kimberly Senior, and Lisa Portes.

I'd like to thank my kids for always being supportive of me and for helping me become a more generous and fun person. My mother not only encouraged me to dream big, but also helped me achieve those dreams. Finally, my wife Jennifer Tanaka has always been my biggest fan and the best partner in the journey through life. I thank her for encouraging me to be more curious about the world.

INTRODUCTION

WHAT DOES A DIRECTOR DO?

If you picked up this book, then you have some interest in directing plays, but maybe aren't totally sure how a director does their job. Maybe you discovered a talent for leading groups of people towards a common goal. Did you see a production and have a hunch that there was another way the show could have gone? Do you read plays and start to visualize them on the stage? Perhaps you tried acting, and you like it, but you are interested in more than one part of the production. I started as an actor, but always yearned to be on the outside of the process, helping guide the whole.

I got my start as a director at the University of Chicago, where I was studying Philosophy full time, but pursuing theatre on the side. My hobby started to take over all my free time as I acted in shows, helped build sets, stage managed plays, and even designed lights. When the school offered an elective in play directing, I followed a hunch and signed up.

I was immediately hooked, loving every aspect of directing. During class discussions, I discovered scenes could mean different things depending on how you read them. The professor brought in professional actors and coached them in a passage from Shakespeare, and I watched his suggestions help the actors find more depth and life in their characters. We students staged our own short scenes for a public showing as the final and I remember investing deeply in making a great piece of art.

As I sat nervously during my scene showing, I remember being outraged when the audience laughed uproariously at certain moments. I almost stood up and interrupted them. Afterward, I remember my professor telling me how happy I should be, because everyone clearly loved the scene. If they were laughing, they were invested, and the best comedy comes from taking the situation seriously. I started thinking of the audience as the final ingredient when directing plays. I couldn't wait to do it again.

This book will harness your hunch about wanting to direct, and help you start to do the job. We'll go through every part of the process from beginning to end, starting with reading a script and ending with opening a play for an audience. For each phase, I'll outline the task, explain one or two methods for accomplishing your goals, and ways to further your studies. In some cases, I'll describe the professional model, to help you understand the potential scope of the director's job. Hopefully by understanding all the little parts that directing a play entail, the entire job will feel exciting rather than scary. I find that each part of the process brings some sense of joy and accomplishment as you head towards opening night in front of an audience.

The book is broken into seven chapters:

- Chapter One: The Role of the Director
  - I introduce a dozen directors from throughout history, examining how they viewed their artistic passion.
- Chapter Two: Reading
  - We dive into finding scripts, reading plays, and preparing detailed analysis to prepare for meetings and rehearsals.
- Chapter Three: Designing
  - I share tips on leading a design process from first meeting to finished plans for set, lights, costumes, and sound.
- Chapter Four: Casting
  - We explore what it takes to prepare for and run effective and fun auditions with actors.

- Chapter Five: Rehearsing
  - Starting from the first rehearsal and moving through staging and scene work, we discover how to help actors build performances and tell a great story. We look at how to bring all the aspects of the production together with clear and dynamic cues during technical rehearsals.
- Chapter Six: Opening
  - Looking at the final few days of the process, we learn the joy of watching the play with an audience, and the bittersweet feeling of walking away.
- Chapter Seven: Devising
  - I offer inspiration for directors who want to create material in rehearsal with an ensemble, creating a production without a script.

The final part of the book offers many practical tools for directing. The workbook provides twenty-one exercises and reminders to help guide the process. Appendixes give examples of some of the ideas covered in the book. A glossary defines helpful terms you use on the job, and the bibliography points you in new directions for study.

This book should help you if you are directing your first two-person scene for class, decide if you want to major in directing in college, or are just curious about the artform. It could serve as a companion to any of your directing classes from script analysis to scene study to collaboration. If you're about to direct your first full-length production, this book can guide you from beginning to end.

In writing this book I draw heavily on research for two other books I wrote: *How to Read a Play* and *How to Rehearse a Play*. Those books were based on over fifty in-depth interviews with working directors from Tony Award winners to academics to experimental artists. In some cases, their advice on how to direct a play contradicts each other, and I share their different views. Part of becoming a director is knowing that there isn't one perfect way to direct a play and that directors refine their rehearsal process over their whole lifetime. I encourage you to find your own way and I try to guide you towards how to make those decisions.

I draw on decades of professional directing and teaching MFA directors at DePaul University in Chicago. Where I think it can help, I offer examples from my own work or what I observe in the classroom. If an idea really sparks your interest, investigate the website or book that I mention. Sometimes a small idea can inspire an entire production process.

I use *A Raisin in the Sun* by Lorraine Hansberry and *The Seagull* by Anton Chekhov as the two main plays that I reference again and again. I find that explaining directing concepts works best when I employ specific examples. I provide summaries of both plays in the appendix, but you might enjoy the book more if you have those two plays handy.

Finally, this book is an introduction to the art and craft of direction. It marks the beginning of an education, not the end. We introduce the basics, but any one of these topics could merit their own book. I encourage you to start the process of being a lifelong learner. Decades into my career, I keep teaching, reading, experimenting, and playing, looking to improve my understanding of how to direct a play.

Throughout this book keep a look out for grey, boxed areas where I ask you to "**Try This**." Think of these as exercises to start practicing the art of directing even before you step into a rehearsal room. Let's start with an exercise right now:

TRY THIS: FIRST THEATRICAL MEMORY

- Try to remember your first memory of seeing theatre.
- What do you recall about the experience?
- Write down anything you can remember.
- Pick a key moment and describe it as fully as you can.

What does this experience tell you about why you love theatre? What aspects of the theatrical experience excite you and stay with you?

Every director we meet in the next chapter refined and revised their process over a long career. They were never satisfied with one idea of directing, but kept looking to answer the question: What does a director do?

1

THE ROLE OF THE DIRECTOR

Why do plays have directors?

A quick historical tour tells us people produced shows for centuries, but they didn't call themselves directors. In fact, the invention of the director is relatively recent—not quite 150 years old. Enterprising leaders created exciting theatrical events, but they didn't call themselves directors.

In Ancient Greece, dramatic poets were focused on winning a playwriting prize, and called themselves teachers as they drilled their actors in the intricacies of their scripts. Around the same time in India the "thread-holder" of Sanskrit drama served as the producer of the event and performed as a sort of narrator and audience guide. In the Middle Ages in Europe pageant managers served as production managers for sprawling productions of biblical stories. Around the same time in Japan, the lead actor of Noh Theatre productions publicized the traditional folk plays, created the masks and props, and worked to maintain traditions. None of these artists called themselves directors.

In England in the late 1500s William Shakespeare led his company primarily through his writing. It's believed actors didn't receive the entire script before opening night, but only their parts. The company would gather a few times to rehearse fights and dances, and on the day of the show played their scenes the best they could. The productions were raucous, noisy, bumpy affairs.

DOI: 10.4324/9781003016922-1

For the next few centuries in England and Europe, plays were produced in this same haphazard manner. Actors would memorize their lines, or in some cases half-memorize, relying on an offstage prompter to help them when they forgot something. The company gathered a handful of times to go over general staging and work on anything that might be dangerous. Actors always marked their performances in rehearsal, meaning they wouldn't put emotions behind their lines and would save their vocal production for the audiences.

If you could go back in time to a production in England in the 1700s you might say—hey these shows could really use a director! The actors don't seem coached at all, and the performers seem disorganized. They don't really seem to be in the same world, some actors think they are in a comedy, others in a tragedy. The costumes aren't telling me a coherent story that matches with the setting and nothing seems based on any kind of historical research. The production is heavy on spectacle and bombastic speaking, light on meaning and impact.

A small number of English actor-managers thought the same thing and worked to reform the profession. Actor-managers took on the lead roles in plays, often Shakespeare, as well as hiring everyone else and organizing rehearsals. They publicized the plays, managed the actors, and designed the sets, props, and costumes. They coached actors to behave more like believable humans, created settings based on historical research, and created performances that were controlled rather than haphazard. They fashioned coherent worlds on stage, trying to convey their understanding of the playwright's intentions.

In the mid-1800s, as the actor manager of the Princess Theatre, Charles Kean strove to improve the quality of productions and create worlds that were grounded in the script, rather than the egos of the performers. Kean spent time analyzing plays deeply, looking for meaning in the text, rather than just opportunities to show off verbal technique. When doing plays set in the past, he did intensive research and tried to recreate historically accurate sets and costumes—in part to unify the world and bring more truth to the stage. He rehearsed plays for weeks and months rather than days, and demanding that actors perform in rehearsal, not just on the day of the show. Kean was heralded for his meticulous work and started to tour his shows to Europe.

The Duke of Saxe-Meiningen, a budding theatrical producer in Germany, saw Kean's work and was impressed by the believability of the acting, the realistic details of the sets and costumes, and the completeness of the world. The duke decided to start his own theatre company, the Meiningen Players, and began to implement all the innovations he'd learned about from the Kean productions.

The duke wasn't an actor or a playwright, but instead someone who stood outside the production, leading all the artists. He championed the play, helped create a consistent theatrical world, coached the actors, and led his ensemble. He researched the play's time period, leading to historically accurate sets and costumes. He strived for realism in all aspects of the productions, from the actions of a crowd to the interpretation of the lead character. He ran rigorous rehearsals for months before showing the work to the public.

The duke directed plays, and we mark his career as the birth of the director.

As we delve more deeply into the Duke's work as a director, we'll examine the roles he filled, the passions he followed, and the jobs he tackled. Then we'll bounce through history examining ten directors in total with the goal of understanding why directors are necessary. What roles did they play? What function did they serve? What were their passions? What did famous directors do and how can we learn from them? We'll look at directors in five categories:

- Director as Creator of Worlds
  - The Duke of Saxe-Meiningen and the birth of the director
  - Yevgeny Vakhtangov and fantastic realism
- Director as Acting Coach
  - Konstantin Stanislavski and the creation of his acting system
  - Viola Spolin and game theory
- Director as Leader of Ensembles
  - Anne Bogart and her Viewpoints techniques
  - Jerzy Grotowski and his creation of poor theatre
- Director as Social Justice Activist
  - Bertolt Brecht and epic theatre
  - Augusto Boal and the spect-actor

- Director as Shepherd of New Works
  - Lloyd Richards and the creation of an African American canon
  - George C. Wolfe and the champions of new work

As you read about each of these famous directors, ask yourself how you relate to what they believe. Do you agree with how they tackled the art of directing? Do you share their values? Do you want to try out some of their techniques? Listen to those hunches and maybe take some notes on your own ideas about theatre.

To begin, let's take a deeper look at the moment when our first director learned that they wanted to change the world of theatre.

THE DIRECTOR AS CREATOR OF WORLDS

THE DUKE OF SAXE-MEININGEN

Before becoming a director, Georg II served as the Duke of Saxe-Meiningen, a small principality in Germany. He was riding high after the Austro Prussian war of 1866, where he successfully led a regiment into every battle. As the German Empire calmed down after the war, the duke focused on what he really loved: the theatre. Why did the duke become a director? When he attended theatre productions, he saw chaos and ego, and felt he could bring artistic rigor and meaning.

At the time, most German theatres threw shows together carelessly, using whatever sets and costumes were on hand. Rehearsals were formalities, devoted to showing off the talents of the star actors, and productions were sloppy. Actors moved where they wanted to haphazardly, and sometimes didn't even know their lines!

After seeing Charles Kean's production of *Hamlet* he researched what was happening in England and took the ideas of the actor-managers to the next level, establishing himself as the first modern stage director. The duke founded the Meiningen Players, recruiting a world class ensemble of artists. He stood outside the production, guiding the designers, the actors, and the technicians towards productions according to his personal vision.

He codified many of the advancements that the actor managers of England had started. He rehearsed for months, and actors were expected to act their roles rather than just mark them from the first day of rehearsal. He worked to dispel star culture; his company knew that in one show you might play the lead, and in the next perform as part of the ensemble. At the time, large crowd scenes were often thrown together with amateurs at the last minute, leading to sloppy distracting messes. The duke believed every moment on stage must be controlled with minute precision, and his crowd scenes became world famous for their beauty and truthful acting.

In the search for the creation of a complete world, he and his designers compiled extensive historical research for each production. They unified their shows around the naturalistic recreation of period settings. If they were doing *Julius Caesar*, they would conduct extensive research on togas, not only clothing each actor in historically accurate garb but tutoring them in how to move and carry themselves like an ancient Roman. The acting complimented the costumes which aligned with the sets, all of which were based on the script.

As the duke led the actors towards creating a complete world, he endeavored to uncover the truth of the script and deliver the playwright's intentions. When he staged scenes, he often talked about motivations. He wouldn't just say move to the left, but instead, "you are drawn toward this character." There are reports of him changing staging on major moments in plays after actors pointed out flaws in his logic. He was always looking for the clearest way to tell the story to the audience.

He published *Pictorial Motion*, one of the first essays on the art of directing. He encouraged directors to sweep audiences into the story of the play by always striving to imitate reality. He advocated creating three-dimensional scenery so actors could interact with the setting rather than pose in front of a two-dimensional painting. He encouraged asymmetry on stage, meaning that there would be more people on one side than the other, because this was truer to life and caught the eye. Actors should work with costumes and props as soon as possible, so they can use them gracefully during performances.

So why did the duke direct plays? He looked around at the amateurish and slipshod productions he observed and thought that theatre could do better. He'd seen evidence that by changing the way rehearsals were conducted, you could improve professionalism and artistry. He believed the main goal of theatre should be to reveal the intentions of the playwright, and he thought that careful reading of the text could help that cause. He believed a single director guiding the production from the outside could create an artistic whole.

His love for theatre paid off and his ensemble created a series of successful productions that gained attention throughout Europe. He decided to tour their work and between 1874 to 1890 played throughout Europe, including Russia, Sweden, Austria, Denmark, Belgium, Holland, and England for over 2,000 performances. Almost every major theatre artist of the early 20th century saw the work and knew the duke had raised the bar.

YEVGENY VAKHTANGOV

Vakhtangov's father dreamed his son would take over for him and become another Russian tobacco baron. But Yevgeny had other ideas. He wanted to be an actor. He escaped to Moscow in 1911 to join the fledgling but reputable Moscow Art Theatre and studied at the feet of the new master of Russian Theatre, Konstantin Stanislavski (more on him in a moment). He dove into new techniques of realistic and truthful acting and was touted as a charismatic and compelling performer. When he grew bored with Moscow Art Theatre productions, he begged to direct his own shows; Stanislavski encouraged his protégé and granted him a studio for experimentation.

Like the Duke, Vakhtangov believed the director's role was to help the entire ensemble create a complete and coherent world. Vakhtangov directed productions that were imaginative, playful, and above all steeped in fantastic realism. In this theory, actors shouldn't play their parts according to how things operate in the real world, but instead based on the new rules the entire ensemble created. Why did Vakhtangov become a director? He wanted to create truthful and playful productions that weren't bogged down in the realistic recreation of everyday human behavior.

Comparing the duke to Vakhtangov is like comparing a photorealistic painter to an abstract artist. The realistic painter uses balance and beauty to create something that tricks the eye into believing they are seeing a slice of reality. The abstract artist uses composition, line, and balance, but their painting of a night sky isn't realistic. The stars don't really swirl—but the abstract painter is after a different truth. Perhaps the abstract painting shows us how we feel about a starry sky rather than what it looks like in a photograph.

Vakhtangov's production of *Erik XIV* by August Strindberg in 1921 at the First Studio of the Moscow Art Theatre showed off his theories of fantastic realism. The play focuses on a Swedish King who refused to wear a social mask to fit in with the rest of society. Vakhtangov directed his king to act like a normal human but guided all the courtiers perform like robots, devoid of human energy. They exaggerated their physicality, and their grotesque makeup and clothes heightened their ghoulish behavior. The production didn't behave like a historically accurate depiction of a royal court, but instead felt like the king's nightmare brought to life.

Vakhtangov debuted his masterpiece in 1922 with *Princess Turandot* by Friedrich Schiller, based on the commedia inspired play by Carlo Gozzi. The play follows the myth of Princess Turandot, who will only marry a suitor who can figure out three riddles. Schiller's adaptation embraces the ancient Italian tradition of commedia d'elle arte in which actors in masks improvise comedic bits around themes.

Vakhtangov filled the production with theatrical flourishes; an actor would fully invest in a dramatic monologue and shed real tears, which a comic would catch in a bowl and show the audience. While the show was meticulously choreographed and rehearsed, actors pretended they were making up their dialogue and improvising their actions in the moment. A chorus of masked performers watched from the sidelines, commenting on the action, and moving the scenery in full view of the audience.

So why did Vakhtangov direct plays?

Unlike the duke, Vakhtangov didn't believe productions needed to mimic reality to create unified worlds. Directors didn't need to research historical epochs and recreate period clothing and behaviors in minute detail. Productions should come from the fantasies of the directors, actors, and designers. Vakhtangov felt emotional truth could be found in the exaggeration of reality through fantasy, theatricality, and playfulness. His created meticulous worlds full of movement, color, and whimsy—worlds that made sense on their own terms.

DIRECTOR AS ACTING COACH

KONSTANTIN STANISLAVSKI

Famed Russian director Konstantin Stanislavski was born in 1863 into a wealthy manufacturing family who loved all forms of performing arts. They reveled in Russian theatre, circus, ballet, opera, concerts, and other cultural events. The parents even built a small stage on the estate where the children staged skits. From a young age Stanislavski acted, wrote, and sometimes stood outside the production to direct his siblings.

As he got older Stanislavski gathered friends and started up amateur theatrical companies, performing a mixture of old classics and new plays. In his memoir, *My Life in Art*, he describes his never-ending quest for "a measure of true feeling" in his own acting. Sometimes, inspiration struck, but often he found himself copying famous actors instead. Worse, he often fell into the trap of ham acting—loud, emotional, and busy performances attempting to dazzle an audience. He spent his entire life looking for the secret to unlock truthful acting.

In the year 1890 at the age of twenty-seven he saw the Meiningen Players tour to Russia and was impressed by the total control the directors wielded. He observed some rehearsals led by one of the Meiningen directors and tried out the dictatorial style he observed. Eventually he tired of controlling actors like puppets and sought instead to put the actor's creativity at the center of rehearsals and performances.

In 1897 he found a like-minded collaborator in the dramaturg and writer Vladimir Nemirovich-Danchenko. Together they founded the Moscow Art Theatre, with the goal of revolutionizing theatre productions. They were faced with the same kind of slap-dash and amateur standards for theatre that had been the norm in Europe for centuries. They vowed to instill their actors with rigor and professionalism through lengthy rehearsals and an insistence on quality over ego. Their first big hit was Anton Chekhov's *The Seagull*, which they rehearsed for months before opening to the public.

Emboldened by the success of *The Seagull* and subsequent productions, Stanislavski spent the rest of his life working at the Moscow Art Theatre, directing, and teaching acting classes. He constantly experimented with new methods in the search for a reliable system of acting. Stanislavski observed that unlike a painter or a composer or a writer, the actor can't wait for inspiration; they need to produce artistic truth on a schedule.

Eventually, Stanislavski gathered his class notes and published his findings. Originally, his works were translated into three slightly unwieldly books in English, but in 2008 Jean Benedetti brought all his writings into one book, *An Actor's Work*. The book reads like an account of a fictional acting class, with a master teacher standing in for Stanislavski and a narrator standing in for all acting students. The first year of the acting class covers "Experiencing" and the second year, "Embodiment." These writings form the core of acting training in almost every conservatory in the Western world.

At the center of Stanislavski's system lies the "Magic If." When working on a role, the actor asks themselves, "If I was facing this set of circumstances, what would I do?" Thinking of the role of Hamlet for a moment:

- If I was a prince
- If my father died under mysterious circumstances
- If my mother married my uncle
- If a ghost came to me and told me to avenge his wrongful death, and
- If I was faced with my uncle.
- *What would I do?*

We will cover this more fully in the next chapter, but you can translate these "what ifs" into given circumstances or unequivocal facts of the script. You can train yourself to be a detective, combing through the play compiling lists of juicy "what ifs" to help actors create compelling performances.

Stanislavski encouraged actors and directors to break the play up into manageable chunks or bits and work on those smaller parts first before trying to act the whole play. You may hear acting teachers talk about "beats." There is a theory that "beats" is just the word "bits" misheard by an American audience not used to a Russian accent. Regardless, Stanislavski encourages actors and directors to start to work on one bit of the play and really understand all the given circumstances and then ask, "What would I do?"

The answer to "What would I do?" is perform an action: the key second part to Stanislavski's system. Acting comes from action, from doing something. You are in conflict over something, you want something but you can't have it, so you perform an action. You do something. We will examine this more fully in the rehearsal section, but one of the great joys of rehearsals is seeing your cast leap into scene work with a sturdy action.

Stanislavski's book contains a wealth of tools for directors to use in coaching actors towards truthful dynamic acting. He saw the role of the director as one who was trying to free the actor to be their most creative self. He has tips on helping actors with concentration, physicality, use of their voice, and backstage etiquette. He covers the control of tempo-rhythm, the development of a creative state, professional ethics, and discipline.

The final section of *An Actor's Work* summarizes Stanislavski's main beliefs about acting and the theatre. He cautions that his system can't be learned in a few hours, but instead takes a lifetime of study and dedication. He says the techniques should be studied, but then completely forgotten when acting on stage in a play.

So why did Stanislavski direct plays? To free actors to do their most creative work. He loved actors and everything about their process from the first steps of discovering a role to the joy of performing for an audience. Stanislavski believed theatre at its core was about human beings, and anything that could help actors embody true human emotions was golden.

VIOLA SPOLIN

Whereas Stanislavski believed actors would need to study for years to be ready to perform, Viola Spolin thought that everyone could act, and anyone could learn to be an actor, without extensive formal training. Her classes, textbooks, and directing stripped rehearsals of heady jargon and dove straight into playing games.

Spolin was inspired by the teachings of Neva Boyd, a social worker who worked at Jane Addams Hull House in Chicago in the early 1920s. Boyd developed the practice of teaching immigrant children games as a way to help them learn. Spolin worked with Boyd and saw first-hand that children could create instant bonds across language and culture when they played together.

Spolin had an interest in theatre from a young age, coming from a large family who put on amateur skits for each other at home. She continued this tradition when she married and had children, gathering with friends to make up theatre games. These evening sessions were some of the first instances of theatrical improvisation that Spolin would try out. She followed her passion, studying acting at the Goodman Theatre in Chicago and with the Group Theatre in New York.

In 1939, Neva Boyd recommended that Spolin lead the Works Progress Administration's Recreational Project in Chicago, and so she returned home to Hull House. Inspired by Boyd's example and faced with students that didn't speak English very well, she started inventing theatre games. Spolin didn't start with a complete training system; when she ran into a problem in rehearsal, she invented a game to solve the issue.

For the next several decades as she moved cities and started different theatres and schools, Spolin increased her stock of games, eventually publishing *Improvisation for the Theatre* in 1963. Spolin declares that anyone can act, and everyone can become stage worthy. Spolin taught people to learn by doing, through games and improvisation. All a leader must do is set the guidelines clearly, let the students play, and then side coach them to follow the rules and be in the moment. Her directing lessons stress that all actors instinctively know what to do, and games and coaching free their natural impulses.

Games include mirror exercises, where one participant moves exactly at the same time as someone else. This game helps build focus, reaction time, and physical listening. Spolin might encourage an entire group to play a game of catch with an imaginary ball while the leader changes the shape, size, and weight of the ball with side coaching.

In 1985 she published *Theater Games for Rehearsal: A Director's Handbook* detailing a thorough rehearsal process based on games. At the beginning, directors play to encourage ensemble, focus, listening, and belief in imaginary given circumstances. Eventually actors improvise movements on an imaginary set, work on stage picture, and share the story with an audience. At every step of the process Spolin encourages the director to empower the actors and to act as a coach and guide rather than rule as a disciplinarian or dictator.

Why did Spolin become a director? For her, directing was a natural extension of her love of teaching and coaching. She saw jargon and the professionalization of theatre as barriers to people experiencing the joy of playing. For her, a director was a primarily a person who should lift people up, encouraging them to discover their innate talents.

DIRECTOR AS LEADER OF ENSEMBLES

ANNE BOGART

In the early 1990s, I was lucky enough to study with Anne Bogart just as she took over the MFA directing program at Columbia University. I remember feeling energized when Bogart put us through our paces in what she called Viewpoints training. She led us through physical exercises, teaching us techniques to move through space and time.

Guided by Bogart, we started moving impulsively, focusing on a single aspect of movement, or Viewpoint. First, we would move only thinking about space, how far we were from each other or the walls of the room. Next, we focused on when we moved, honing our timing through kinesthetic response. Slowly Bogart exposed us to architecture, tempo, duration, and other Viewpoints. Finally, we improvised with all the Viewpoints at once, whirling like modern dancers.

When I impulsively moved with the rest of the students, I was amazed at my physical freedom. I didn't need to think about where or how to move; my body knew. I felt present and alive, senses heightened to the group dynamic. When I stood outside the group, I was stunned by how everyone created compelling visual pictures and dynamic movement sequences, all without anyone guiding them.

In *The Viewpoints Book*, Bogart, with co-author Tina Landau, explains how she first learned about Viewpoints from choreographer and experimental director Mary Overlie. Through Viewpoints, performers and directors could create work that emphasized the physical over the intellectual. They could allow space, time, and shape to lead the way instead of the usual suspects of story and character. The Viewpoints allow actors and dancers to create freely, allowing their instincts to take over.

Bogart heralded Viewpoints as a method for creating ensemble. As actors work together, they learn to communicate on a level beyond the spoken language. Viewpoints can be used to create an ensemble for a specific show or build bonds within a permanent theatre company. She let us students know that she'd been working with Viewpoints for years with her theatre group, the SITI Company.

When we went to see the SITI production of *The Medium*, the company members dazzled the audience with their physical dexterity and impeccable timing. The company devised the play, based on the writings of the media guru, Marshall McLuhan, coiner of the phrase, "The medium is the message." I still remember scintillating moments from the show: a perfectly synchronized line of actors gliding across the stage, McLuhan stuffed impossibly into a small table, and a hilarious TV Western spoof.

The Medium kicked off a thirty-year collaboration between Bogart and her SITI Company. The actors and designers spent years training in Viewpoints as well as the Suzuki movement method. In her seminal book, *A Director Prepares*, Bogart extols the virtues of working with a resident company of actors over many years. As they work together, they develop a shorthand. They push each other out of artistic habits, and explore new ways of making theatre. The SITI Company taught their methods in summer intensives in residencies at universities, and in special workshops.

So why did Bogart become a director? She saw herself as a leader of an ensemble, someone who could be their first audience. She wanted to explore a movement-based kind of theatre, one that could experiment with how to stage plays and devise projects. She wanted to work with the same people again and again, believing she could take the work farther if she didn't have to start from scratch each time with a new company of actors and designers.

JERZY GROTOWSKI

After World War II, Poland fell behind the Iron Curtain, one of the many communist states essentially under the control of the Soviet Union and Joseph Stalin. While this was not great for the political freedom of young theatre enthusiast, Jerzy Grotowski, it did allow him to travel easily to study at the Moscow Art Theatre. He steeped himself in the theories and techniques of Stanislavski and Vakhtangov as well as other revolutionary theatre makers. While Grotowski wasn't interested in the psychological realism and naturalism of Stanislavski, he was inspired by the Russian master's insistence on experimentation and the search for truth.

In 1965 he established a theatre company in Wroclaw, Poland naming it the Theatre Laboratory. He inspired his ensemble to undertake decades of theatrical research. Grotowski was less interested in creating hit productions than in the long, slow process of experimenting with theatrical forms, trying to understand the essential power of performance. After the devastation of World War II and the horrible process of reconstructing Poland, artists wondered how to make pieces that mattered. Why make theatre? How should they make theatre? What should it look and feel like?

Grotowski and his Theatre Laboratory asked the question: What do we need to make theatre? Do we need sound? No. Theatrical lights or costumes? No. Do we need elaborate sets and props? We don't. All that is needed for theatre to exist is an actor and a spectator. They obsessed over the encounter between performer and audience. They called their work Poor Theatre, embracing the lack of physical materials, focusing on the actor's body and voice.

As outlined in his book, *Towards a Poor Theatre*, Grotowski invented a new training method that stressed the physical over the psychological. He led his ensemble through rigorous exercises to develop complete control over their muscles, their skeletons, and their movements. They developed breathing techniques to open their vocal channels, transforming the whole body into a resonator. They even developed "facial masks" in which they held the face in a certain way to mimic old theatrical masks.

Grotowski rehearsed for months or even years with his ensemble in creating theatrical pieces. One of their most famous was *Akropolis*, in which they used an old polish epic poem that centered on Bible stories and transposed the action to the Auschwitz concentration camp. The piece feels as much like a ritual or an exorcism as a play, using chanting, physical toil, extreme physical motions, and ensemble movement to evoke the horrors of the Holocaust.

You can find a recording of this historic production online and marvel at the precision and commitment of the small ensemble. The audience surrounds the actors, sometimes sitting only inches from where they sweat, strain, and howl. The performers seem like they are almost possessed by demonic spirits rather than acting. Grotowski drove them to search for the emotional truth of each moment, and to fully express that truth with their whole body and voice.

Why did Grotowski become a director? What did he think about the director's role? Grotowski valued lifelong experimentation with a committed group of actors over any sense of commercial success. He saw his role as provocateur, teacher, guru, and spiritual advisor to his group. For Grotowski, the journey mattered much more than the destination.

DIRECTOR AS SOCIAL JUSTICE ACTIVIST

BERTOLT BRECHT

Bertolt Brecht came of age in Germany during times of great social and political unrest. He was a young man during the horrors of World War I, and saw his country badly beaten and punished for their hubris. As the country struggled to rebuild itself, Brecht noted with alarm the rise of Adolf Hitler and his rabid National Socialist party. To avoid being arrested as a political outsider, Brecht fled the country in 1933 and lived in exile. While abroad in Switzerland and America, he created some of his most famous plays, each centered on different aspects of the political realities he faced. After the horror of the Second World War, Brecht returned to what was now known as East Germany in 1949, working for the rest of his life behind the Iron Curtain.

As an artist of his time, Brecht believed strongly that all theatre was political, and the role of the director was to create works with a message for the masses. In *Brecht on Theatre*, translator John Willet compiles the director's theories over a lifetime. In a short manifesto from 1944, Brecht says that theatre shouldn't be judged by how many tickets it sells, but by how it motivates people to change the world.

Brecht wrote the plays he directed, which always examined people's relationship to power, money, class, and society. *Mother Courage* depicts a woman who slowly loses her family and her humanity as she tries to survive in the Thirty Year's war. *Three Penny Opera*, written with composer Kurt Weill, compares the merchant class with a band of criminals. Sometimes Brecht used an old fable, such as *The Caucasian Chalk Circle*, to examine current social ills.

Brecht believed theatre must teach audiences political lessons, which was impossible if they were sucked up into the story. Brecht attempted to alienate the audience from what they were seeing, using different devices to cause the audience to consider the economic and societal forces at play. Patrons should never forget they were in a theatre and should be able to view the events with a critical eye.

German innovators such as Erwin Piscator had introduced what they called Epic Theatre; a method Brecht eagerly embraced. If narrative theatre emotionally manipulates the audience through storytelling, epic theatre encourages viewers to think clearly for themselves. Epic theatre encourages audiences not to identify with the hero, but to judge them and analyze their actions.

Brecht used different techniques to achieve his alienation effect. Sometimes he started a scene with a projection or title card that explained what the audience was about to see. Sometimes he drained the acting of its emotional content and had actors face out and speak directly to the audience. He inserted songs into the middle of scenes, juxtaposing something lighthearted with a cruel dramatic moment.

In a book put out by his Berliner Ensemble in 1949, Brecht outlines his typical process from beginning to end—it mirrors some of the work we'll be discussing throughout this book. When the director first reads a play, they seek out key moments to underline for social significance. Once he knows why he's launching the production, Brecht analyzes the script and goes into rehearsal and design. Just before the end of the process, Brecht schedules what he calls a "checking rehearsal" where the director makes sure the social significance of all the important moments are landing.

Why did Brecht work as a director and writer? He saw his role as a political provocateur. He wouldn't let any moment rest until he had turned it over to figure out how to make sure his message landed on the audience. No moment in the show was beneath his laser focus, and his productions inspired political theatre makers for decades to come.

AUGUSTO BOAL

Augusto Boal also grew up in tumultuous times, threatened by his government, and created political theatre in response. In the late 1960s the Brazilian military dictatorship ramped up their reign of terror on citizens. At the time, Boal led the Arena Theatre, making more and more adventurous work that criticized the ruling party. In 1971 Boal directed a play by Bertolt Brecht, *The Restable Rise of Arturo Ui*, a thinly veiled critique of the rise of authoritarianism. On the way home from the theatre one night, government agents kidnapped, arrested, tortured, and eventually exiled Boal to Argentina.

While in exile, Boal published his first book, *Theatre of the Oppressed*, arguing that theatre should take one step beyond Brecht's alienation effect to politically energize theater goers. Audiences shouldn't just watch plays but take an active part in them. His troupe performed a scenario of political oppression and then paused the action, asking the audience to make suggestions about how the scene could play out differently. Boal gave the audience power to turn a scene of domination to one of liberation.

Boal tells the story that one night an audience member was frustrated with how the actors were executing her suggestions and she stormed on the stage saying she would just do it herself. Boal proclaimed the birth of the spect-actor. No longer should audience members sit in their seats, either identifying with the characters on stage or judging their actions. Instead, they should make their own theatre, get involved in the action, and rehearse the political revolution.

After the fall of the military dictatorship, Boal was able to return to Brazil in 1986 and set about engaging working class spect-actors in the power of theatre. He held workshops, created traveling shows, and worked with non-trained actors to explore political and societal issues. In his book *Games for Actors and Non-Actors*, Boal lays out exercises to help anyone express themselves, find their voice, and move their body in theatrical ways.

Why did Boal become a director? Boal saw himself first and foremost as a theatre maker who represented the poor and the disenfranchised. He believed theatre could rally against injustice and train people to find solutions for their problems. He made theatre to liberate people from their oppressors, starting with the oppression of being a spectator.

DIRECTOR AS SHEPHERD OF NEW WORK

LLOYD RICHARDS

Growing up as a working class Black man in Detroit in the 1930s, Lloyd Richards had very few role models in the arts. He originally went to college to study law, but the theatre department drew him in. He abruptly switched majors, studying all aspects of stage craft. In 1947 he moved to New York City and started acting, directing, and teaching studio classes for actors. One of his students was Sidney Poitier, who rose to be the most celebrated Black actor of his time.

Poitier recommended Richards direct the world premiere of Lorraine Hansberry's play *A Raisin in the Sun*, a production that changed theatre history. The play broke all sorts of barriers, as the first show written by a Black woman to be produced on Broadway. It ran for 530 performances, introducing many white audiences to the inner family life of Black Americans for the first time.

Richards was hired a year before rehearsals began, allowing Hansberry and Richards to meet once a week to discuss the play and investigate rewrites. Drawing on what he learned from

Hansberry, at the first rehearsal Richards told the cast their job was to accurately portray the life of a Black family on stage. Afterword, Hansberry told him he'd captured the essence of her play. In interviews, Richards held this compliment up as the highest accolade. He believed the director's job was to simply reveal what the playwright has to say.

As the show started previews in Chicago, Hansberry was forced to leave town on personal business. At this point, she trusted Richards enough to let him run the production and get daily reports over the phone. Each night, Richard would give her his impression of how the show went, and she would make changes to the script. Eventually, the show moved to New York, opening to standing ovations and history-making accolades.

In 1969 Richards was appointed as the head of the National Playwrights Conference at the Eugene O'Neill Theater Center, a company that exclusively develops new plays. In interviews, Richards extols the virtue of canonical plays by Shakespeare and others, but he makes the case that every classic play was new at one point. New plays contribute to the ongoing reflection of a culture, and without allowing them to go through a period of trial and error, we won't ever create new classics.

At the O'Neill Richards developed a lasting process for cultivating new work. He installed dramaturgs as the liaison between the director and the playwright. Plays were given four days of rehearsal, and always performed script in hand. New play workshops throughout the country still follow the basic outline set up by Richards. Famous playwrights such as John Guare, David Henry Hwang, Wendy Wasserstein, and August Wilson all were developed by the conference during his time.

Playwright August Wilson submitted his plays to the National Playwrights Conference five times but was continually rejected. Finally, he sent in what was to become his first big hit, *Ma Rainey's Black Bottom*. Richards personally took on the project, beginning a decades long collaboration with Wilson. Richards immediately connected to Wilson's project of chronicling Black life in Pittsburgh and felt he'd met all the characters at one point in his life.

When Richards worked with Wilson, he strove to understand his motivation for writing the play. In this way Richards helped Wilson achieve his vision, prodding him towards rewrites. He never told Wilson what to write but gave advice and asked questions. Richards would go on to direct the premiere productions of six of August Wilson's world-famous plays.

Why did Richards direct plays? On one hand, his entire life focused on lifting the work of playwrights eager to chronicle the Black experience in America. In a larger sense he strove to help any new writer find their voice, through workshops, dramaturges, and guidance. As a producer he believed that the future for American Theatre lived in the imaginations of living playwrights. Throughout his life, Richards saw himself in service of something larger than himself, stewarding young talents in all aspects of theatre.

GEORGE C. WOLFE

Growing up Black and gay in Kentucky in the 1950s, George C. Wolfe, like Richards, didn't have many artistic role models to follow. He overcame many obstacles to become a famed writer, director, film maker and producer. He directed landmark productions on Broadway including the Tony award winning production of Tony Kushner's gay epic *Angels in America* and the tap dance infused *Bring in 'Da Noise, Bring in 'Da Funk*. He served as artistic director of the famed Public Theater Company in New York City from 1993 to 2004. He faced discrimination in his childhood, which led to his desire to open as many doors as possible for others when he had the chance.

In interviews, Wolfe outlines his different roles in the theatre. In his words, writing is an art, directing is a craft, and producing is a job.

When he's writing, Wolfe tells stories that haven't been heard before, igniting audiences with compelling ideas. When he started in the business, he didn't see Black plays that he wanted to direct—he craved theatrical and fantastical narratives. His first big hit, *The Colored Museum*, a review-style show, deals with everything from the horrors of slave ships to the comedy of talking wigs.

As a director, Wolfe says his job is to discover the rhythm of the show. He says that the most primal thing we respond to—not language or even sound—is rhythm. Audiences surrender to pulses almost automatically. Laughter, applause, and even silence help shape the rhythm. Every piece he directs flows differently, and to discover the rhythm Wolfe tries to uncover the urgency at the heart of the play. Why did the writer have to write this piece? What drove them? In these investigations Wolfe believes he'll find the most dynamic rhythm for the production.

As a producer Wolfe opens doors for everyone he possibly can. He searches for people who have something to say, typically writers who haven't had their stories heard before. In his eleven years as the producer at the Public, he championed playwrights who would eventually go on to have major hits on Broadway and shows that would enter the modern canon of plays. He emboldened writers such as Lisa Kron, Suzan-Lori Parks, and Tony Kushner.

Why did Wolfe become a producer and a director? When he was first hired to be the producer at the Public Theater, he talked about gaining more power, not for the sake of power itself, but so that he could continue his exploration and growth as an artist. And as the producer of one of the largest non-profit theatres in the country, he created a structure where many different people—people of color—could tell their stories. As a director, he searches for the specific blueprint to success for each script, knowing that every play is different.

THE ROLE OF THE DIRECTOR

Each of these directors responded boldly to the world, reacting to the society they grew up in, and the theatre they witnessed. They believed theatre could change the world, by creating community or fostering political ideas or creating beauty. They started working to fill a void and create something new.

I introduce these ten directors so that you can understand the history of our craft, discover the origins of the ideas we are investigating, and encourage you to learn about yourself. Why do you want to direct?

Flip back through each of our directors from history and ask "Do I see myself?"

Do you identify with the directors who were creating theatrical worlds with their complete visions? Are you drawn to the historical research and detail of the Duke of Saxe-Meiningen? Do you thrill to hear about the fantastical universes the Vakhtangov created? Are you more excited about coaching actors and helping them build indelible performances? Have you been exposed to the ideas of Stanislavski already? Do you find yourself inspired by looking for given circumstances and actions? Are you more drawn to the game play of Viola Spolin and her vision for a world where anyone can act?

Do you see yourself working with an ensemble of friends and fellow artists like Anne Bogart or Jerzy Grotowski? Are you intrigued by building a physical world through choreography and improvisation? Are you drawn to scripts, or do you want to devise your own new work? Do you think your work will be inherently political, drawing audiences to bald societal realities like Bertolt Brecht? Or like Augusto Boal will you go one step further to involve the audience in the show itself?

Do you have a desire to work with a playwright closely like Lloyd Richards? And help new voices be heard by audiences? Or do you think you're drawn to classic works? Does the life of George C. Wolfe inspire you? Are you hoping to be a producer of sorts, bringing together groups of artists to create something new?

If you think you want to do everything above and more, that's exciting. Or you may not know the answer to any of these questions right now, and that's completely fine as well. If you feel any urges towards a type of theatre, I encourage you to investigate further. It's not too early to start asking yourself, why do I even like theatre? What parts of directing excite me? What role do I think I could fill right now?

TRY THIS: WRITE A MINI MANIFESTO

- Think about productions you loved. Do they have anything in common? Style? Content?
- Think about plays you hated. Why? What turned you off?
- Have you experienced any amazing rehearsal rooms? What worked?
- Any moments in rehearsal that felt off? Why?
- Think about the world you live in right now. Can theatre do something to make it better?

Write out a few thoughts on these questions and ask yourself: What kind of rehearsal would I like to run? What kind of plays would I be proud to produce? Why do I like theatre?

SUMMARY

In this chapter we have introduced:

*   The birth of the director
*   The role of the director
*   A very brief history of ten influential directors
    *   The Duke of Saxe-Meiningen: creation of a complete world
    *   Yevgeny Vakhtangov: fantastic realism
    *   Konstantin Stanislavski: creation of an acting system
    *   Viola Spolin: games to teach actors
    *   Anne Bogart: Viewpoints techniques for ensemble
    *   Jerzy Grotowski: creation of Poor Theatre
    *   Bertolt Brecht: epic theatre and the alienation effect
    *   Augusto Boal: empowerment of the spect-actor
    *   Lloyd Richards: the creation of an African American canon
    *   George C. Wolfe: the champion of new work

FURTHER READING

For an overview of many of the directors mentioned here, as well as contemporary directors, you can turn to the collection of theatrical writing edited by Toby Cole and Helen Krich Chinoy called *Directors on Directing: A Source Book for the Modern Theatre*. There are two books that compile interviews of modern directors, both called *The Director's Voice*, the first complied by Arthur Bartow and the second by Jason Loewith.

I've mentioned many of the books by and about these directors in the chapters above, but I'll put them all here for easy reference. The life and theories of Yevgeny Vakhtangov is compiled in *The Vakhtangov Sourcebook*, edited by Andrei Malaev-Babel. Konstantin Stanislavski's incomparable book on acting is best read in the version titled *An Actor's Work*, translated by Jean Benedetti. Benedetti has written many short and clear books about Stanislavski, including *Stanislavski and the Actor*, *Stanislavski: a Life*, and *Stanislavski in Rehearsal*. Viola Spolin has two easy to digest books on directing and acting: *Theatre Games for Rehearsal: A Director's Handbook* and *Improvisation for Theatre: A Handbook of Teaching and Directing Techniques*. Anne Bogart has written many influential books including *The Viewpoints Book* and *A Director Prepares*. Bertolt Brecht's theories, writing, and history can be found in *Brecht on Brecht: The Development of an Aesthetic* edited and translated by John Willet. Brecht's plays have all been translated into English, including *Mother Courage*, *The Caucasian Chalk Circle*, and *Galileo*. Augusto Boal's theories are contained in *Theatre of the Oppressed*, and his games and technique are compiled in *Games for Actors and Non-Actors*. George C. Wolfe's many plays have been published including *Spunk*, *Jelly's Last Jam*, and *The Colored Museum*.

HELPFUL WEBSITES

Some of the directors and their theatre companies have websites devoted to their work and theories:
www.mxat.ru/english
www.vakhtangove.ru/en
www.violaspolin.org
www.siti.org
www.grotowski.net
www.imaginaction.org

Some theatre companies still exist that the director from this chapter either led, or worked at exclusively:
www.publictheater.org
www.theoneill.org
www.berliner-ensemble.de/en

2

READING

THE MAGIC OF READING PLAYS

Why do we read plays?

Plays open a world of possibilities: perhaps you learn about a culture you know nothing about, and the story transports you to a new world. Maybe an ancient play set in a foreign country teaches you about your own time and place. Does a brand-new play speak to this moment? Did you empathize with the characters, leaving your own reality, and submerge yourself in someone else's story? Playwrights create fictional universes that carry you into their world. Who are you on the other side of that journey?

As a director, you may read a play you want to realize on stage. In weeks, or months, or even years from this moment you'll sit in the audience and watch actors speak the dialogue, fleshing out the playwright's world. In the next few chapters, we track the director's process from reading, to analyzing, to casting actors and designing the world, to rehearsing, and finally opening the play to audiences.

As you read this chapter, I encourage you to think of yourself as a director. When you choose to read a play, you make the first directorial decision—selecting a project that needs to be seen right now. You start reading through the lens of the director's craft. I divide this chapter into four sections:

DOI: 10.4324/9781003016922-2

- Choosing plays and gathering first impressions
- Learning about the play through close reads
- Dividing the play into sections and understanding action
- Summing up your point of view

Directors read, re-read, and then read again. They write down evidence, scribble ideas, and dream up images. They let the script wash over them and dig into individual sentences. They work alone now, so they can confidently lead collaborations in the future.

First, let's focus on a potentially magical moment—the first time you read a play.

COLLECTING IMPRESSIONS FROM FIRST READS

When you first read a script, you have the chance to experience a play the way an audience does: for the first time in real time.

Try to guard the experience as a sacred event. Turn off all cell phones and other possible distractions. Find a comfortable place to sit and read the play straight through. If the play has an intermission, take a break and think about what you just read. Are you hooked? Do you want to get back to see how it turns out? Read the second act. Write down any first impressions or questions. Don't think about this too much, jot down anything that comes to mind. Who are you drawn to? What surprised you? What do you love about the world, the language, the themes? How were you affected emotionally by the end of the play?

If you read a play and don't respond to it—or just plain don't like it—trust those instincts. I've been torn in the past when a theatre company has approached me with a play and asked about my interest, but I really didn't like the script. I always try to be honest and tell them that I appreciate the interest and love their company, but this script isn't for me.

If you love a play on a first read, keep those feelings close to your heart. As you move forward with the production your ideas will deepen through interactions with your collaborators and more thorough study.

CHOOSING A PLAY

Let's take one step backwards. Before you experience the magic of a first encounter, you first must choose a play. As a student, teachers will assign you plays from many eras. You may find that one of your assignments turns into a passion project. Or perhaps reading a play by an author you like sends you to the library to sift through all of their published works. As a director, I encourage you to move past your homework assignments and start reading on your own. Start to figure out your taste and find projects you might love to direct.

You could begin with the theatrical canon: plays that stand the test of time and are produced decades or even centuries after their opening nights. Some canonical playwrights include Sophocles, Euripides, William Shakespeare, Moliere, Anton Chekhov, Henrik Ibsen, Arthur Miller, and Tennessee Williams. The canon also includes plays written by Black, female, Latinx, LGBTQ, Indigenous, Asian, and other artists. If you're interested in these voices, check out Adrienne Kennedy, Li Xingdao, Kalidasa, Aphra Behn, Zeami Motokiyu, Sophie Treadwell, and Zora Neale Hurston.

Maybe you're interested in new plays by women? In 2014 a group of playwrights and publishers created The Kilroys to champion new female writers, typically underrepresented on stages. Every year since 2014 the group publishes a list of plays at their website that features highly recommended, unproduced plays by women, trans, and non-binary authors. The website lists the play, the cast size, and a summary. Some writers have profiles at The National New Play Exchange (NPX). By paying a small annual fee, directors have access to thousands of new plays, including one-acts and ten-minute scripts.

Another way to discover new plays and playwrights is to read reviews of productions throughout the country. New York City is the country's largest theatrical market, so keeping track of what's premiering or being revived each season will provide scores of titles. But don't be afraid to look in other theatrical markets such as Atlanta, Chicago, Seattle, or Baltimore. You could only focus on productions in London and Australia and never run out of material to explore. Remember that traditional newspapers can sometimes overlook smaller theatre companies, so seek out blogs or alternative press to make sure you're finding out about the most diverse array of artists.

ENCOUNTERING SCRIPTS WITHOUT READING

What if you know that you are a kinesthetic learner? Or that you understand best when hearing things out loud? What if you don't love reading plays?

While I think directors can't escape some reading when it comes to preparation for meetings and rehearsals, you can engage with plays through other methods. If you're looking at classic plays, there's a decent chance you can find an audiobook version. Audible has a huge and growing selection of plays, both classic and new. You'd also be surprised how many titles are available through public and school libraries. With an audio version of the play, you can listen to the material while you go for a walk or do your laundry. If you allow yourself enough time you can experience the play straight through from beginning to end.

If you can't find a recording, gather a group of friends to read the play out loud. Perhaps you could organize a monthly event where you read a script or two, or selections from plays, with a discussion afterward. Many theatre companies pick their seasons this way. They might have a committee of people who are reading plays, sorting out likely contenders for their company, and then eventually lining up a few readings.

When you listen to plays out loud, you can follow the same exercise as when you're reading a play. Try to encounter the play as an audience member. Experience it for the first time. Jot down your impressions or talk them out with colleagues.

In this first phase of reading, you're looking for scripts, finding writers you love, and reading a play that excites you. Now that you've read the play once, it's time to dig in more carefully. It's time to read like a director.

TRY THIS: MAKE A LIST OF DREAM PROJECTS

- Grab a notebook or create a digital document and start a list of plays.
- Go back through any syllabi you've had, and mark plays or playwrights you loved.
- Dig through theatre websites you like and write down titles that intrigue you.
- Head to The Kilroys, Alternative Canon websites, or other compilation sites.

Can you start a list now of plays you love, plays to explore, and dream projects? Do you see any patterns emerging about your taste? Do you want to carve out time once a month to read new plays or reexplore classics?

AMASSING DETAILS FROM CLOSE READS

By performing script analysis, we move beyond our first impressions and start to discover how a play works.

A typical audience member won't scrutinize a play as they're watching it; the events wash over them in real time. But ideally every member of a production team analyzes a script before starting work. A set designer reads the play, trying to understand each of the settings and discover what props are needed. A costumer digs through the play to get a sense of characters and what they might be wearing. An actor pores over a script to discover their emotional journey.

Directors are guided by Stanislavski's advice on how to coach actors: "If I was faced with this situation, what would I do?" We read first to understand the facts of the play, and then we uncover how the characters react. We will examine:

- Given circumstances—how to spot them, how to research them, and what to do with them
- Action—decoding what happens and finding a pattern that makes sense

As you begin your studies I recommend writing out as much of your analysis as possible. Committing something to paper helps you understand your thinking more clearly.

DETECTING GIVEN CIRCUMSTANCES

As a reminder, a given circumstance is something we know is true from the text of the play. It's a fact and it's undeniable.

Why do we read through the play to find facts? In part to help guide actors to grounded performances—they need to believe the fictional given circumstances and then act. In *A Raisin in the Sun*, why does Walter Lee start the play out wound up and bitter? Look at his history—he's a limousine driver without many prospects, he lives in the apartment he grew up in as a kid, and he saw his dad work for decades without much to show for it. The more we know about his past, the more we can understand why he acts in the present.

We also learn details about the setting through a close read. In a first quick study of the script, we may not pick up on every detail about the small apartment that the Younger's cram into, or the new neighborhood they might try to move to. These details about place can help our understanding of the design of the play, and further explain character motivations.

In her book, *The Director's Craft*, Katie Mitchell outlines a very thorough method for amassing given circumstances. She encourages directors to take out two pieces of paper and on one write Facts and on another Questions. Start reading slowly from the beginning and write down any facts you know to be true about *things that happened before the play began or places that exist*. If you were looking at Loraine Hansberry's classic *A Raisin in the Sun* from the beginning, you'd start to amass the simplest of facts just from the dialogue.

Walter Lee Younger and Ruth Younger are married.
Walter and Ruth have one child, Travis.
Travis sleeps in the living room of the Younger apartment.
There is a common bathroom in the hallway that is shared by several apartments.

> Last night Walter and some friends were talking in the living room after ten p.m.

You'd also start to ask some questions:

> How long have Walter and Ruth been married?
> How long have they all lived in this apartment together?
> Is today's morning routine different than any other day?
> How common was it for Black families to live in small quarters on Chicago's South Side?
> Is the Younger apartment based on any true to life apartments?
> Where on the South Side of Chicago do the Youngers live?

As you read further, you may find that some questions are answered later in the play. You can cross them off your questions list and put the new information into the fact column. Walter's mother reveals she's been living in this apartment ever since she was married, which implies that she's been living in this apartment for almost thirty years, and both Walter and Travis have lived here their entire lives.

At this point, avoid opinions about characters or situations. *Walter is disappointed with his lot in life.* This may be true—but we can't establish it as a fact and it's also a pretty general statement. There may be parts of his life that he loves fully; we just don't know yet. *Ruth nags her husband.* Again, this is an opinion, and one that really judges the character of Ruth. Yes, she may encourage him to stay on time and push him to be realistic, but the word nag comes with negative connotations. Also, there are many places that Ruth supports and loves Walter, and we don't have a clear sense of what is habitual and what is out of the ordinary today.

Why do we start with events that happened *before the play begins?* Because great characters don't exist just when they are on stage, they have deep personal histories. We want to know everything about these people before the play begins. Who are they when lights come up on the first scene? Once we know who they are in the beginning, we'll have a better understanding of how they change over the course of the play.

TRY THIS: TRACK GIVEN CIRCUMSTANCE

- Pick up a play you've studied or read before.
- Start to read very slowly from the first page.
- Write out any facts you are sure about.
- Jot down any questions that occur.

At the end of the first scene, ask yourself, what did you learn? How do you view the play differently? Do you know the characters better than when you started?

INVESTIGATING QUESTIONS

After reading through the entire play very slowly, you'll amass a huge list of facts about things that happened before the play began. Read them over. You'll understand what events shaped the characters more clearly. Your list of questions may even be longer! Cherish these questions as an opportunity to learn more about the play and to start making some decisions.

As you read through the questions you can typically divide them up into three categories.

Questions about living conditions and job prospects for Black families on the South Side of Chicago in the 1950s can be answered through careful and thorough research. Look for books about housing and economics as well as race relations. Also dig into Lorraine Hansberry's personal history. As a young child she lived through a situation very similar to the events depicted in *A Raisin in the Sun*; while the play isn't strictly autobiographical, knowing what Hansberry was drawing from can answer some questions. If I have a dramaturg, I assign these questions to them, while also doing my own research.

You might question the specific timeline and relationship history after a first read. Sometimes you can learn what you need through a second or third read through of the play. Questions about when Ruth and Walter met and when she moved into the apartment may not be definitively answered by a second read—but we can infer that they moved in as soon as they got married. Questions about when exactly Walter's father died may seem obscure at first, but after a second pass may become clear. If I have an assistant director, I like

Type of Question	Process for Answering	Who is responsible?
History, dramaturgy, playwright life and times.	Research	Dramaturg & Director
Backstory, relationship, timeline of events.	Re-reading	Assistant Director & Director
Character motivation, specific moments.	Rehearsal	Actors & Director

Figure 2.1

to assign these questions to them, to get them to read the play more deeply. I'll also try to answer them myself.

Some questions are best left for the rehearsal room—especially those about character motivations. After reading the play many times I may still wonder exactly why Walter eventually refuses the offer of more money from Lindner. If you answer this question before you get in rehearsal, you'll cut the actor out of the process.

Finally, don't worry if you can't answer all the questions. A great play contains mysteries that can never be answered by a production but are left for each audience member to ponder long after the show closes.

EXAMINING STAGE DIRECTIONS

Stage directions are usually set off from the dialogue of the play and describe physical things such as props being used, or actions that the characters take.

Are they facts? Should we read them as given circumstances? I encourage you to think of stage directions as proposals from the playwright: examine each one and decide if it speaks to your production.

On the first page, Hansberry declares the action takes place on Chicago's South Side between World War II and 1959. I'd suggest the time and place are given circumstances and should be put down in the facts column. These two facts lead to many questions: *What were living conditions like on Chicago's South Side after WWII? What neighborhoods did Black families live in and why? What jobs were available for Blacks in Chicago in the 1950s?*

Hansberry also describes the Younger's apartment carefully: the kitchen is connected to the living room and dining room area, there is an alcove where Walter and Ruth sleep, there's only one other room that is through a doorway. These facts lead to questions: Where are the doors on the set? What size are the rooms? What kind of furniture do they own? What is the condition of the furniture?

Hansberry also provides detailed character descriptions. Are these facts? Think about three famous productions of the play: Denzel Washington, Sidney Poitier, and Sean Combs brought Walter Lee to life in very different ways. When I read a detailed description of a character, I tend to put these in the questions category: *Is Walter lean? Why would that be? What does Hansberry mean when she says he's "intense and full of indictment?"*

You've read through the play carefully, amassing a list of facts about the characters and the setting. You've dug into research to flesh out what you know about the play and examined the stage directions to see what else you can learn. By now you have a pretty good grasp on the magic "What Ifs" of the script. Now it's time to turn to action: what do the character do?

THE ACTION MAP OF THE PLAY

While scripts consist of dialogue and stage directions, plays are made of action.

One of the great joys in the theatre is to learn about a character through their action, what they do on stage. When Walter tries to excite his wife about buying a liquor store and she says to eat his eggs, what does he do? When Mama tells Walter that his wife is pregnant and considering getting an abortion, what action does he take? When he's lost all his money in a swindle and his dreams seems gone, how does he react? Being in the room live with characters as they make choices thrills an audience. Plays are made up of action.

Another way to think about dramatic action: what changes? If one character wants something from someone else, either they will get what they want or they won't but regardless—some sort of change will happen. Characters make decisions and the course of the play alters.

You can track dramatic action by asking what is different from the beginning of the play to the end. At the beginning of *Raisin*, the Younger family is expecting a check for $10,000 and aren't sure how to spend the money. By the end they've decided to take the risky but empowering step to move into a house in the white neighborhood of Clybourne Park.

To understand how you get from the beginning to the end, examine smaller units of action. Ask yourself, how is the end of act one different from the beginning? At the top of the play, Beneatha hopes some of the money will go to her medical school tuition. Walter plans to make a down payment on a liquor store. Mama doesn't know what she'll do with the money, but by the end of the first act she decides to buy a house. Why? What happens in act one that drives her decision?

Once again you can drill down to a smaller unit to find the clues. Start looking at the scenes of the play and ask—what's different from the beginning to the end? If we look at the second scene of the first act, at the top of the scene Mama discovers that Ruth is pregnant and is considering getting an abortion. At the end of the scene when she tells Walter this news, he seems to have no answer. Mama decides that her family is falling apart, and she must make a change.

Break down the play into the smallest bits and discover what happens.

BREAKING THE PLAY INTO BITS

How can you divide a play into bits that are easier to understand? Start by marking exits and entrances. Who is on stage at the top of the play? Now, when does another person join them? Does someone leave? Every time someone enters or exits, the dynamics shift. You've just started to figure out the French scenes of the play.

In the 17th Century, French farces were known for their surprise entrances and exits, and playwrights broke their plays down based on who was on stage. We've adopted this term and now we say that every time someone enters or exits marks a new French Scene.

By flagging every exit and entrance in a script you learn a lot about the rhythm of your production. How often will the audience be jolted by a new character or an exit? Are there a lot of short French scenes in one part of the play? Are there longer scenes between characters in another? What do you learn from this structure?

Now that you have all your French scenes, ask yourself the same question we asked about acts and scenes: what is different at the end from the beginning? What changes? What happens in this section of the play?

In a short French scene, what happens might be very simple. A character learns that the hallway bathroom is clear, and they rush out of the room to get ready for work on time. Other French scenes are more complicated and should be divided even further. See Appendix 3 for a French Scene breakdown of *A Raisin in the Sun*.

TRY THIS: CHART FRENCH SCENES

- Go through your play and mark every entrance and exit.
- Create a table with character names on the left and French Scene numbers on the top.
- Put an X in the box every time someone is on stage.

What did you learn about your play? How many short scenes are there? Where are there long scenes with more than a few people? What is the entrance and exit rhythm of your play?

TRACKING EVENTS

Sometimes you'll look at a longer French scene and realize, wait, more than one thing seems to happen in this bit. It seems like the scene starts to go one way, and then changes direction. Maybe it changes more than once. You've started to discover dramatic events.

An event is a change that happens onstage that affects every other character and alters the course of the play. By marking every exit and entrance, you've already marked many of the events of the play. If two people on stage are joined by a third, the new character interrupts what they were doing and spins the scene in a new direction.

Discovering dramatic events within scenes takes some practice. Look for those moments where the scene takes a turn, where if that choice wasn't made, the play might take a different course. If a long-married husband tells his partner, "I love you," this most likely doesn't mark an event. If a young lover declares, "I love you," to their beloved for the very first time, their action marks an event. The dynamics of the scene changes. What will the other person say? Do they feel the same way? Are they excited to reciprocate? Or do they want to escape? Dramatic events create moments of uncertainty.

In the first scene of *A Raisin in the Sun*, Walter tries to convince Ruth to spend the coming insurance money on a liquor store and she puts him off. He keeps trying new tactics to get her interested: he excites her about his plans, he appeals to her maternal instincts, he encourages her to dream big about financial success. Finally, Ruth grounds her husband in reality, "Walter, leave me alone." She takes a moment and then says, "Eat your eggs, they gonna be cold."

The tone and mood of the scene changes immediately. Walter stops bugging Ruth about his plans and instead complains more bitterly about not feeling supported in his dreams. Ruth switches tactics as well and tries to encourage him to think realistically. The scene changes because Ruth finally snaps.

Go through the entire play and mark each dramatic event and label them simply. For example, *Travis exits to the bathroom. Ruth tells Walter to leave her alone and eat his eggs.* Now read these over, you'll start to have a sense of what happens in the play. You're starting to understand how characters affect each other over the course of the story and what decisions they make. You'll start to notice patterns. In some scenes there are many entrances and exits and dramatic events one after another. In other places scenes take more time and stay on the same topic for longer.

Now that you've broken your play into smaller bits, started to uncover the actions of the play, and discovered what people do: now it's time to pull back and examine the entire structure. Now you can create an action map.

MAPPING THE ARCHITECTURE OF THE PLAY

In the mid-1800s, German dramatist Gustav Freytag created the dramatic pyramid for analyzing scripts. He based his model on a traditional analysis of plot and action. He challenges readers to identify the hero of the story or the protagonist and then follow them as they navigate a series of crises. Mapping the action map of the play

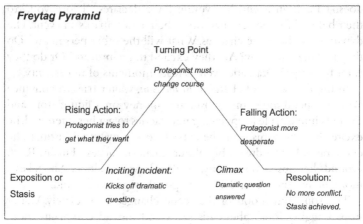

Freytag Pyramid

Turning Point
*Protagonist must
change course*

Rising Action:
*Protagonist tries to
get what they want*

Falling Action:
*Protagonist more
desperate*

Exposition or
Stasis

*Inciting Incident:
Kicks off dramatic
question*

Climax
*Dramatic question
answered*

Resolution:
*No more conflict.
Stasis achieved.*

Figure 2.2

should help you tell the story of a play with excitement, as you follow the twists and turns of the plot.

Let's unpack *A Raisin in the Sun* as we identify the following key moments in dramatic structure:

- Status Quo
- Inciting Incident
- Rising Action
- Turning Point
- Falling Action
- Climax
- New Status Quo

The status quo describes the calm before the storm at the top of the play. We open on the Younger family living in a cramped apartment, awaiting a $10,000 insurance check. Walter has been meeting with his friends about a plan to invest in a liquor store—but no definite decisions have been made. What will happen?

The inciting incident lights the match that sets the play on fire. Beneatha forcibly tells Walter that the money is Mama's to invest, and she'll never put it in something she finds sinful. Now we have conflict. What will Walter do? At this moment we ask the dramatic question, "Will Walter achieve his dreams of independence and self-worth?" We'll track Walter's progress towards this goal for the next three acts.

The rising action tracks Walter as he tries to achieve independence and self-worth by convincing the rest of the family that his scheme to open a liquor store is worthwhile. In scene after scene, Walter tries to reason with is family, cajole them, browbeat them, and implore them, but is rebuffed again and again.

We hit the turning point at the top of the dramatic pyramid when Mama let's Walter know that she's invested a good portion of the money in making a down payment on a house. She picked a house in a white neighborhood because it was the only one she could afford, despite the likely prejudice the family will face. Mama's action upsets Walter and he shifts course from trying to convince his family to join him to going behind their back and stealing some of the money.

After the turning point, we start to track the falling action: Walter completely defies his family, thinking only of himself. Walter loses the money he'd taken from Beneatha when a shady conspirator runs off with his cash. Then a white member of the neighborhood where Mama put a down payment on a house comes to the family to encourage them not to move. He offers to buy them out and give them even more money.

We've hit the climax. Walter says he'll take the money even if he must debase himself in front of a white man. In a bold move, Mama says that Walter can make the decision for the family, but he must do it in front of his son. The dramatic question comes to a head: will Walter achieve his dream of independence and self-worth? The white man comes to the door with a check, and we all wait with bated breath—what will happen?

In a surprise move, Walter forcibly turns down the neighborhood representative, asserting that as a proud people they can't take his money. They can't be demeaned, and Walter tells Lindner to leave. The dramatic question has been answered, but not in the way that we expected. Walter has found a way to find independence and self-worth but has done so by reuniting with his family and seeking a different kind of dream: the dream of home ownership.

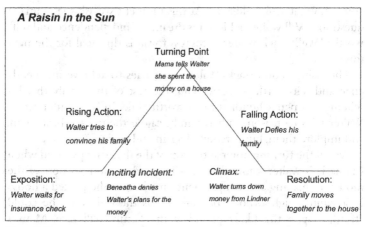

Figure 2.3

We reach the final stage of our dramatic analysis: new stasis or the new status quo. This is what we've been fighting about the entire play. Now the family is reunited in spirit and start to furiously finish packing for their move.

CHARTING THE MOST IMPORTANT MOMENTS IN THE PLAY

Now that you've looked at all the entrances and exits, charted the events of the play, and discovered the action map, I encourage you to perform one more bit of analysis: the moment chain.

In his compact and helpful book, *Tips: Ideas for Directors*, Jon Jory suggests that not every moment in your play will be as important as every other moment. Some moments will stand out, grab the audience's attention, and hopefully stick with them after the play. He suggests directors create a moment chain of the twenty-four most important events that deliver the narrative and emotional heart of the story.

Why twenty-four? In my experience this isn't a magic number, but rather a good suggestion for a typical two act play. It means there's an important moment every few pages. When I assign this task to my students I suggest if they are working with a ninety-minute, one-act play they choose eighteen and about thirty for a three-act play.

What is a moment? A moment is an event, a decision, a turning point—typically bracketed by some physical action or perhaps a meaningful pause. When looking for moments, avoid choosing an entire scene—look for the instant or the short exchange.

In *The Seagull*, the entire performance of Constantine's play wouldn't land as a moment; you probably won't remember that entire sequence. When Constantine stops his play because his mother is making fun of it, this moment should resonate and reverberate for the rest of the evening.

The key moments in the first act of *The Seagull* (See Appendix 4 for a complete list of moments) are:

- Constantine shows Sorin his stage
- Constantine and Nina Kiss
- Nina is revealed and the play begins
- Constantine stops the play, yelling at his mother
- Everyone pauses to listen to singing across the lake
- Masha declares her love for Constantine to Dorn

These moments set up the main story: Constantine loves Nina and wants his famous mother to embrace his artistry. Masha loves Constantine, but he rejects her. The lyrical moment when all the characters stare across the water listening to faint music captures the beauty of the lake, the longings of the characters, and the interconnected web of relationships.

We'll come back to the moment chain in the design chapter, using this tool as a guide to check our work.

DEVELOPING A POINT OF VIEW

So far, you've found a play that you loved on a first read, and you jotted down your first impressions. Then you took some time to understand the backstory of the play and got a clearer handle on the characters. You broke the play into manageable bits and charted the action of the play from the largest moments to the smallest. Now, how can you summarize what you've learned? How can you translate your deep knowledge of the play to any possible collaborator?

Lisa Portes, Head of Directing at The Theatre School of DePaul University, has developed a simple rubric for her students to fill out that helps them home in on the center of their production. She asks the students six questions:

- What is the play about?
- What kind of play is it?
- What is the dramatic question?
- What is the spine of the play?
- What do you want to do to the audience?
- What is the cry of the play?

Let's walk through each question as if we were imagining a production of *The Seagull*, by Anton Chekhov.

WHAT IS THE PLAY ABOUT? *UNREQUITED LOVE*

Start with your hunches about the play when you first read it. If you think about all the characters and what they want and all the events in the play, what idea or theme do they center around?

I chose *Unrequited Love* because it seems like every single character in the play yearns for someone who doesn't love them back. Some characters even have unrequited love for the arts; they love the theatre, but the business doesn't seem to love them back.

WHAT KIND OF PLAY IS IT? *A DARK COMEDY WITH A TRAGIC ENDING*

Konstantin Stanislavski directed one of the most famous productions of *The Seagull* for the Moscow Art Theatre in 1898. He and Chekhov famously argued over the production because even though the title page declares *The Seagull: A Comedy in Four Acts*, Stanislavski's production was slow and somewhat brooding.

Armed with this knowledge, the first three acts strike me humorously. These characters' longings and desires are slightly hysterical and over the top. They want love and appreciation so badly; we can't help but laugh. When I get to act four, it's hard to sustain this comic tone.

Be creative here: is your play a comic book political thriller? A Black-Mirror type satire? A dystopian nightmare comedy?

WHAT IS THE DRAMATIC QUESTION? *WILL CONSTANTINE RECEIVE AFFIRMATION AS AN ARTIST?*

We ask the question at the inciting incident and answer it at the climax. In the case of *The Seagull*, the big moment of Act One occurs when Constantine stops his play after his mother keeps making jokes. He's outraged by her disrespect and storms off. At the end of the play, after discovering his mother hasn't even read his published writing, and after his muse Nina says she still loves Trigorin, Constantine spends two minutes ripping up all his manuscripts and walks off stage to shoot himself. Sadly, the answer to this dramatic question is no.

WHAT IS THE SPINE OF THE PLAY? *TO SEEK VALIDATION*

Harold Clurman, author of *On Directing*, developed the idea of the spine of the play out of his studies of the acting principles of the Moscow Art Theatre. Clurman and his Group Theatre modeled their work in the 1920s and 1930s after Stanislavski's acting principles. Craft the spine with a simple sentence that captures the action of the script. What does the main character strive for in every scene? What is at the heart of the play?

In the case of the *Seagull*, in almost every scene characters seek validation of some sort. They desire the love of someone who shuns them, or they crave applause for their work, or they simply seek recognition for their labors.

WHAT DO YOU WANT TO DO TO THE AUDIENCE? *MAKE THEM LAUGH WITH RECOGNITION IN THE FIRST ACTS AND CRY IN THE LAST*

This question moves from the internal to the external. If you're working on a satire, you'll likely want the audience to laugh grimly at the proceedings. If you're working on a tragedy, you'll want to bring the audience to some sort of catharsis.

With *The Seagull*, I know that laughter is a way to endear audiences to characters, so I hope audiences will fall in love with the hapless residents of the lake house. I hope they laugh because they see themselves on stage. Once they are pulled in, I hope to break their hearts in the last act as everything that seemed funny before has curdled.

WHAT IS THE CRY OF THE PLAY? *WE NEED TO VALIDATE OUR YOUTH—ESPECIALLY OUR YOUNG ARTISTS*

Portes describes the cry of the play as the burning message she hopes audience members will think about after they leave the theatre. What burning question sits at the center? What hidden message seeps through every page?

You have a chance here to express your personal vision. Again, look back at your notes from your first reading. What pulled you emotionally? Why do you think the play needs to be seen? Why does it need to be performed for your specific audience? Every single director who directs *The Seagull* will stage the events of the play in order—only you will have your personal take on why this script is necessary right now.

ANALYSIS THROUGH READING OR BY DOING

For some directors, the most effective way to learn about a play isn't through reading the script over and over, but instead through hearing the play and working on it in some format. Perhaps by having a workshop period before the official rehearsal begins where directors can collaborate with actors and possibly designers. They can learn about dramatic events, structure, and given circumstances together. They can read a scene and then discuss with the participants: what did we learn? What happened? What questions do we have?

The advantage to this method is that plays are meant to happen out loud, in real time, acted out by people. When we read plays alone, we have to imagine how the scene will sound. We make decisions or figure things out for ourselves, without the input of others.

In our next chapter, we'll learn how to collaborate with others on the production, expanding how we view the play.

SUMMARY

In this chapter we have explored:

* First reads
* Choosing a script
* Given circumstances
* Research on the play and playwright
* Diving a play into French Scenes
* Discovering dramatic events
* Looking at the dramatic structure
* Creating a moment chain
* Answering six key questions

FURTHER READING

Many books on directing have robust sections on script analysis and play reading, and there are a few that focus strictly on reading plays.

One of the most succinct and clear books on understanding plays is *Backwards and Forwards* by David Ball. The rigorous Katie Mitchell goes into detail on how she amasses and works with given circumstances in *The Director's Craft*. Brian Kulick's *The Elements of Theatrical Expression* will point you towards the building blocks of theatre that are hidden in all texts.

There are also many textbooks on script analysis including *Script Analysis for Actors, Directors, and Designers* by James Thomas, *Page and Stage: An Approach to Script Analysis* by Stanley Vincent Longman, *Introduction to Play Analysis* by Cal Pritner and Scott E. Walter, and *How Plays Work* by David Edgar.

My own book, *How to Read a Play*, is based on interviews with over forty working directors and offers many ideas on how to analyze scripts. It ends with twenty-one exercises for reading plays.

HELPFUL WEBSITES

Places to look for new plays and new ideas for classics.
www.thekilroys.org
www.newplayexhange.org
https://sourceful.us/doc/454/alternative-canon
https://www.americantheatre.org

Websites that offer readings of plays:
www.playingonair.org
www.audible.com
www.latw.org

Theatrical Rights companies
www.concordtheatricals.com (formerly Samuel French)
www.playscripts.com
www.dramatists.com
www.broadwayplaypub.com

3

DESIGNING

The preliminary work of a director is somewhat solitary and mostly theoretical. In the early phases of the production, you work alone to find a script you love and figure out how to talk about it. Your research into the playwright, perhaps done with a dramaturg, helps you understand why it was written. Analyzing the given circumstances and the dramatic structure gives you a sense of how the play might work.

Now you start to imagine the physical world of the play. I'm going to walk you through a typical design process, which may be more advanced than you will run at this stage of your career. Any time you can emulate what happens in the profession, you'll elevate your work and prepare yourself for a life in the theatre outside of school. Regardless of the level of production support or the number of resources at your disposal, in this chapter you'll learn how to:

- Develop a point of view around design
- Collaborate with team members
- Move from abstract ideas to practical solutions

Discussions with collaborators challenge your ideas about the play. You create plans for the set, choose costumes for the characters, and guide the sound and lighting designer towards creating a world.

DOI: 10.4324/9781003016922-3

In this chapter I take you from the theoretical to the pragmatic:

- Assembling the creative team
- Running the first design meeting
- Leading a concepts meeting
- Refining designs with your team

When directors work on the design of a show, they need to balance two impulses: the desire to control everything and the impulse to let your collaborators do their work. If you don't give any parameters or direction, your team won't know where to go. They will respond better to a clear idea of the shape of the sandbox and the toys they can play with rather than an open beach. On the other hand, if you just dictate what you want from beginning to end, you'll never hear the great ideas designers cook up. If you don't give them room to breathe, they won't be able to act freely as artists. I encourage you to start each meeting from a place of curiosity and mutual respect.

ASSEMBLING THE CREATIVE TEAM

In the professional world, as soon as the director is hired, they start to hire the designers and production team. The director's task in this phase is to assemble a creative team that they think will work well together, serve the needs of the play, and get the job done. A director will rarely get everyone they want, so they need to be ready to make substitutions and work collaboratively.

If you're working in a conservatory setting, it may be that you have no choice over your designers as they are assigned to your show by department heads. In this situation, see if you can find a time to get a coffee with each of your collaborators to build camaraderie. You might ask them how they got into design, what they like about theatre, what they think about the school. Any shared reference points will allow you to start the first meeting from a place of common ground.

You might be working in a theatre department where there are no designers. Perhaps you've been given permission to do the play, a space, and some time, but not many other resources. What should you do in this situation?

I highly recommend you try to recruit some friends to join your show and work as designers. As we've already seen, a director holds many responsibilities in a production. They must figure out a point of view, guide collaboration, help build a fictional world, and manage the many people involved. It will become increasingly hard to direct the play if you're pulling the costumes, writing the sound cues, hanging the lights, and building the set.

Do you have a friend who always knows how to dress? Might they be interested in costuming others? Do you know anyone obsessed with music? Could they be corralled into designing sound for your show? Who is the most organized person you know? Maybe they are a budding stage manager and don't know it yet.

Directing a play is similar to working as an entrepreneur in charge of a small, startup business. You have a vision for a final product, and you need to bring people aboard to join the project. If you can provide a clear sense of purpose, belief that their opinions matter, and a sense of accomplishment, you'll give each of your collaborators a great gift.

THE ROLES ON THE CREATIVE TEAM

Let's go through some of the key roles on the creative team. Knowing what each person does will help you assemble the right squad.

- Set Designer
  - Conceive of every physical aspect of the stage set. They set the ground plan, determining where any walls, doors, furniture, or drapes will land. They either create technical drawings themselves or work with a technical director.
- Costume Designer
  - Imagine what every character will wear throughout the play. They design the color palette, keeping in mind what the set looks like behind them. They run costume fittings with the actors, making sure everything looks right and works well with what the actor is doing in the show.

- Lighting Designer
  - Conceive of how the lights will look overall and then home in on each scene to determine the mood, tone, shape, time of day, and atmosphere. They create a lighting plot, determining where lights should be positioned so they can illuminate the set and the actors.
- Sound Designer
  - They either pull or compose all the sound effects and music used for the show. Some sound effects are called for in the script: cars pulling away, gunshots, storms. They also pull or compose music for before the beginning of the play, intermission, and scene transitions. They may provide music for underscoring scenes.
- Stage Manager
  - Makes sure the production follows all the rules and regulations of the actors' union or the theatre company or school. Once in rehearsal, they keep the room organized and on track, keeping the schedule and managing communication between all the departments. Once in technical rehearsals, they call the lighting and sound cues (and projections and scenery cues if appropriate). They work as a main artistic collaborator with the director in creating a safe and positive rehearsal room.

If you're lucky enough to have a few people to choose from for each position, have discussions with some of the candidates and talk about the production. Do you have any ideas about how you'd like to work together? Do you want to talk about process? How might they work on the show? What are they looking for from a director? If they've read the play, you can talk a bit about the show and gather some general ideas about what they're thinking about.

You might even look at some images or listen to some music together and discuss. Do you have the same taste? Do you find the same things beautiful? Finding your artistic partners will make the process more fulfilling and exciting.

TRY THIS: CONDUCT IMPULSIVE RESEARCH

- If you can find some magazines to cut up, leaf through and pull out any images that resonate with your play. Don't think too much about this.
- If you can't find magazines, do some simple image searches based on the themes of your play and see what you can find.
- Go through music you love and start to create a playlist for your show.
- Try to not be too literal with these searches—but find things that speak to the ideas and conflict in the play.

What patterns do you find in these collages? Are there colors, lines, shapes that jump out at you? What tone does the music suggest for you? What other impulsive research can you conduct? Do you want to do some drawings? Make a sculpture?

LEADING THE FIRST DESIGN MEETING

Now that you assembled a creative team, it's time to start the design process.

If you can, I encourage you to gather all your key designers for the first meeting. By meeting all together you avoid miscommunications. You progress farther as a group when you all start on the same page. Also at these meetings, you feed each other. The set designer will be inspired by the sounds they hear, the lighting designer will learn about the colors of the costumes. Your goal is to get everyone speaking the same language about the play: one you discover together.

The first meeting sets the course for discovery and covers practical details. Design meetings are always one part artistic dreaming and one part pragmatic scheming. At the first meeting try to cover three essentials:

- What is your point of view on the play?
- What opportunities does the script offer?
- What are the given circumstances of this production?

In the professional world, these meetings often happen online over Zoom or Google Meet. If possible, try to get everyone in the same physical room—you're sure to make more connections.

POINT OF VIEW

In preparation for this first meeting, you've read the play many times and analyzed the structure. Look back at the work we covered in Chapter 2 and see how you can turn those ideas into prompts for designers. At a first meeting they will turn to you at the top and expect you to say a few words.

Why are you drawn to this play? Why does it need to be seen here and now? Glance over your list of given circumstances, trusting your instincts: which ones jump out at you as the most important? Trust your vision and know that if you tell the story of the play filtered through the unique way that you see the world, you'll create a compelling production.

One way to pull all this information together is to go back to your six key questions. Looking back at my answer for *The Seagull*, I can transform my analysis into guidance for designers:

- *What is this play about:* Unrequited Love
  - Probably we want to build an intimate world so we can focus on the many love triangles in the play.
  - This world is full of passion and that should be reflected in the design.
- *What kind of play is it:* a dark comedy with a tragic ending
  - It's key that we signal it's okay to laugh right from the beginning. How will we capture this comic tone in the lights, sound, costumes?
  - What transformation should we try to create to make a different tone for the last act?
- *What is the dramatic question of the play:* Will Constantine receive affirmation as an artist?
  - Let's talk about that play within a play as a group—what impact should that have on the audience? Does Constantine have talent or not?
  - The play ends with Constantine ripping up his manuscripts, how do we make sure that moment lands?

- *What is the Spine of the play:* To seek validation
  - This play is about artists, wannabe artists, and artist group-ies. What does that world look like, feel like, sound like?
  - Do people dress to impress? What type of looks do people adopt to try to make an impact?
- *How do we want to affect the audience:* We want them to laugh in the first three acts and cry at the end
  - We probably already covered this, but worth mentioning again that Chekhov thought this script was a comedy and so do we.
- *What is the cry of this play:* We should validate our young artists before it's too late
  - This cry brings our play into the here and now. Young art-ists everywhere are clamoring for change—how can we echo those cries in our production?

I ask as many questions as make assertions in my first remarks to designers. I try to make clear to my collaborative team that there are some things that I know, some things that I don't know, and some things I have a hunch about. I'm trying to point in the right direc-tion, without prescribing how the design will be solved.

After these brief remarks I open it up to the rest of the room and ask any number of questions to get the rest of the team speaking:

- What do you love about this play?
- What resonated for you?
- What questions do you have?
- What excites you about the work?
- Where are you nervous or what challenges to you see?

As you listen to your designers during this first meeting really try to hear their interpretation without judgement. Do their ideas sur-prise you and stretch your understanding of the play? Encourage collaborators to unpack their opinions. Great ideas can come from anywhere. Are there any similarities from people that you want to highlight? Any differences worth exploring? By talking through two opposing points of view, a group may finally come to a better under-standing of an issue.

In their book *Notes on Direction*, Frank Hauser and Russel Reich gently advise directors: "Don't expect to have all the answers." They suggest there are only three responses to any question: yes, no, or I don't know. I tell my students be sure you answer any questions your designers ask truthfully. If a designer asks you a question that you don't know the answer to, don't try to fake your reply to look smart. The best answer probably is, "I don't know, what do you think?"

WHAT OPPORTUNITIES DOES THE SCRIPT OFFER?

Every play creates a unique world. As you sit down with your team for the first time, try to identify some of the key artistic opportunities the script offers. What's special about this play? What puzzles will you solve as a group?

Consider the setting of your play. Does your play take place in one location or many? Is the setting realistic or poetic? Do you need many props and set pieces to tell the story or almost none? Consider some different kinds of plays and their challenges.

Single Set: *A Raisin in the Sun*

The entire three act play takes place in the Younger's apartment. The Younger family has lived in this cramped space for decades and the apartment is almost like another character. You'll need to do research to create a 1950s South Side Chicago apartment. You'll also need to create a ground plan of entrances, exits, furniture, and rooms to help create flow and spur the action of the play. How can you get across the years of living these walls have seen?

Many Locations: *Hamlet*

Hamlet calls for various locations in and around the royal castle of Denmark. The ramparts, the Queen's bedroom, a gravesite, a royal chamber, and many more. In the original script, Shakespeare didn't indicate settings, scenes ended when people left the stage and began when new characters entered. The plays were performed in the Globe theatre, with audiences surrounding the stage on all sides.

If you were doing *Hamlet*, would you mimic the Globe Theatre and create a single setting that is transformed by actors and lighting? Or do you want more concrete settings for each scene with thrones, tables, chairs, and other set pieces? How fast do you want the transitions to move? How will you accomplish this?

Four Distinct Settings: *The Seagull*

The Seagull takes place in four locations on Sorin's estate: a parkway, a croquet lawn, a dining room, and a study. When Chekov's play opened at the Moscow Art Theatre a curtain rose, revealing a complete set of some sort. At the end of the act, the curtain lowered, and the crew changed the set. Audiences had time to eat some food and get a cocktail. When they returned to their seats, the curtain rose again revealing a completely new setting.

How will you transition from one location to another? Do you want to create something that's more modular so that the transition from one place to another is more seamless? How realistic do you believe these settings need to be? Will you have three intermissions?

Multiple Realities: *She Kills Monsters*

Qui Nguyen's action-packed comedy concerns an English teacher whose younger sister dies in a car crash, leaving behind her Dungeon's and Dragon's module—a sort of blueprint for playing the fantasy role playing game. The teacher decides to play the fantasy game and in a theatrical gesture, is thrust into her sister's game—befriending elves and demons, fighting monsters, and leading an epic quest. Half of the scenes take place in the mundane modern world: kitchens, classrooms, living rooms, hallways. The rest of the play moves in the fantasy universe: magical caves, enchanted forests, and treacherous mountain sides.

How can you create two distinct worlds that somehow work together? The everyday scenes should feel mundane, while the fantasy scenes should pop with excitement—how do these two worlds co-exist in one play? How can you move seamlessly from one to the other?

During this first meeting with your designers talk about challenges and opportunities. Start to think about the world you are creating. Is it fluid and ephemeral or hard and sharp? If there are multiple settings, how will we move from one to another? Is there a way to contain the whole? Is there one metaphor that speaks for your entire play?

WHAT ARE THE GIVEN CIRCUMSTANCES OF THIS PRODUCTION?

In some ways the design process for a Broadway production and a low-budget amateur show in a found space are the same. The team starts the first meeting with a script, a theatre, a budget, and through the course of meetings figures out how to design the set, costumes, lights, and sound. But of course, there are huge differences in terms of the resources. During the first meeting clarify limitations, opportunities, and levels of support.

Some of the biggest determining factors are:

- Theatre space
- Budget
- Time
- Support team

Probably the best way to proceed is to ask a lot of questions as a group.

Theatre Space

How large is the space you are working in? Is there a lot of room for set pieces as well as room backstage for more to come on? Or is the space more modest? What scale will you be working at?

What relation will the audience have to the play? Will they surround the play on two or three sides? Will they be able to see each other? Will they all see the same view? Will it feel like a picture far away or an experience right in their laps?

Budget

It's not the director's job to manage the budget, but they should have a sense of scale. Get a sense from your designers early on about the level of complexity you can afford.

Will characters be able to have multiple costume changes to help tell story or will we be mostly focusing on one or two looks? Can you realize the set in minute detail? Or will you make a big gesture with a few pieces? Will the amount of lighting instruments allow for an infinite variety of looks and colors? Or should you try to home in on some key looks?

The budget is simply another given circumstance, like the play, the theatre space, the cast, and the designers. How can you work smartly with the materials you have? As my colleague Lisa Portes says—you are always dealt a hand of cards on every production. How can you play the cards you have well rather than wishing you have a different hand?

Time

How much time is there from the first meeting to the beginning of rehearsal? If you only have a few weeks, jump quickly to practical choices. If you have months to go you can spend more time talking theoretically and about theme and vision.

Be sure you understand the basic structure of meetings. How often will you be meeting? Are these set ahead of time, or will you need to schedule them now? What deadlines does the theatre company or department have for the designers? When do they need to have preliminary and then final designs?

If there isn't a set structure of meetings and designs, set one soon with the help of a production manager, stage manager, or someone else in the department or theatre company. Clear expectations help people create with a sense of freedom.

Level of Support

How much are designers expected to do on their own? How much support will they have from others? Is the costume designer, on their own, to do all the shopping, fitting, sewing, and alterations? Or do they have an army to support them? How about the lighting designer? Are they on their own to hang, focus, and cue all the lights? Or do they have assistants and electricians?

It's not your job to manage these positions or even to really know about every single person working on the show. But if you know that your designers are doing most of the work themselves, try to figure out together the realistic expectations for the end product.

WRAPPING UP THE FIRST MEETING

At the end of the first meeting, summarize what you talked about and set goals for the next meeting. Remember we covered three important aspects:

- What is your point of view?
- What opportunities does the script offer?
- What are the given circumstances of this production?

Perhaps reiterate some of the common vocabulary that you discovered. If you all agreed on some of the challenges and exciting problems to solve for the show, talk those over and get people thinking about possible solutions for the next meeting. People should have a clear sense of the direction of the production, the practical boundaries they are working within, and the next few steps of their work.

Agree on what people will be doing before the next meeting. If you have a generous amount of time, then typically people will compile picture and sound research. They will return to the next meeting with a set of images, photos, sounds, music clips and other bits of tangible research that represents where they are heading.

TRY THIS: MAKE AN OUTLINE FOR A FIRST DESIGN MSEETING

- What is your point of view on the play?
- What is the story in a simple paragraph?
- What do you want to hear from your collaborators?
- What are the specifics of your production?
- What are the steps for the next meeting?

What did you learn about your show by making this outline? How can you create structure for discussions, while allowing for true conversations?

LEADING A CONCEPTS MEETING

Ideally a few weeks later, you'll have your second gathering: the concepts meeting.

Designers show their initial research and share first ideas about where they are heading. Set, Costume, and Lighting designers share photo and artistic research. These photos might show a concrete image of a possible costume or prop, or they may just evoke a feeling. Sound designers bring in evocative music or sounds.

On viewing a designers ideas, I ask the rest of the team to comment first about what they see and hear. What do they like? What do they have questions about? Encourage some conversation. If you speak first, you may not learn anything from others. When you do weigh in, be clear, specific, encouraging, and probing.

What do you like? Why? What specifically about the color or shape makes sense to you? What details speak to the character or the situation of the play?

Many directors I interviewed found sifting through research clarifies their understanding of the characters and the story; especially when they see a picture they don't like but can't at first articulate why. By being honest—"No that seems off, but I'm not sure why," they start a conversation. By eliminating one look for a character, they start to articulate who the person is and how they operate. By steering away from a picture that doesn't resonate, they help collaborators home in on a common language.

WHAT TO EXPECT FROM EACH DESIGNER

COSTUMES

Costumers typically present image collages for each character. If they work on a show set in the past, they might need to go to the library and find clothes catalogs or magazines from the period.

Looking at a collage for *A Raisin in the Sun*, you might see a typical chauffeur outfit, as well as leisure wear for a thirty-year-old Black man from the 1950s. Another set of images presents what a female college student would wear. The designer walks through their research, pointing out what was typical for the time and what purpose each garment served.

Clothes help an audience immediately categorize a person. At a glance you might be able to understand a character's:

- Class
- Status
- Taste
- Profession
- Age

And there might be even more abstract qualities you could gather from looking at clothing:

- Color might indicate a person's emotions
- Fabric choices could suggest the way the person thinks
- Silhouette might illustrate how they move

SET

Depending on the size of your budget and the type of play you are working on, set design research might be granularly specific or more evocative. If you are working on a single, realistic set like *A Raisin in the Sun*, likely the photo research will be of apartments on the South Side of Chicago in the 1950s. The designer might bring in pictures of kitchens, living rooms, furniture, wallpaper, and layouts. They might also bring in photos of the outside of the building and street even if these will never make it onto the stage but only provide context.

If you're working on something that has less specific historical needs like *Hamlet*, the images may evoke a feeling or a theme. If the team has decided that the show is about a renegade trying to find their way in an autocratic world, perhaps the designer will bring in photos of various dictatorships throughout history.

LIGHTS

The lighting designer will likely show images that range from the atmospheric to those that depict a specific place, time of day, or season. Eventually lighting designers will be working with instruments hung in the air or placed on the ground, pointed specifically at the stage. In the planning phase they are thinking about:

- Angle
  - Is the light imitating the sun in the sky? Or some sort of interior fixture?
  - Is the angle drawn from real life or trying to help establish mood?
- Color
  - Natural light has many shades depending on time of day, cloud cover, season, and even location.
  - Indoor lighting has different shades depending on the type of instruments.
- Practical lighting fixtures
  - Maybe a real lamp on stage is the best way to light the scene.
  - Instruments can be fashioned to mimic fireplaces, candles, torches, and campfires.
- Intensity and coverage
- Quality and tone
- Emotional impact

Lighting design sets place, time of day, and season. In these early sessions, it's important to make sure you're all on the same page. If a scene is set on a dark chilly night, you want the costumes, lighting, acting, and sound design to all complement each other.

SOUND

Sound designers in this early phase might bring in different types of music to sample, which serve as inspiration for transitions or possible underscoring. They may play examples of sounds they like. Talk about how sound will work in the show. Music and sound set the mood and tone of a scene. Will the beginning of the play sound different than the end?

If your show transitions between scenes, you'll want sound, music, or a combination of the two to transport us from one place to the next. Some plays may benefit from having sound or music under scenes to help establish place, time, and mood. Engage in general conversations now, knowing you might change your ideas once you are in rehearsal or tech.

TRY THIS: STUDY THE ELEMENTS OF DESIGN

- Flip through a magazine or perhaps a fashion website—focus on the clothing—what do you learn about each person because of the color, line, fabric?
- Find a book or a website about architecture—examine the spaces—how does the type of material and angles of a room impact you?
- Walk around your home and just observe the light in each room—where does it come from? What quality does it have?
- Listen to a random assortment of music—what changes the mood of a song? Tempo? Instrumentation? Melody?

What did you learn about the different aspects of design? How can you train yourself to see the impact of different design choices on mood and tone? What non-verbal information did you pick up from your experiments?

MOVING FROM THE THEORETICAL TO THE PRACTICAL

As you move from vision, to concepts, to practical designs, take time to check your progress against your initial analysis. You might change some of your original ideas based on suggestions from your designers. Remember your main job is to tell the story of the play, and highlight moments that align with your evolving point of view.

Think about the last act of *The Seagull* and how many practical choices you'll need to make as a group before you start rehearsing the scene. The last act takes place in a small room that has been converted into a study. The weather is horrible outside, and people have gathered to say goodbye to Sorin, who is now quite ill.

When you first explore this scene with your designers, ask some basic questions based on your initial analysis:

- The first three acts are comedic, but the last is tragic, how will we show that change in the lights, sets, and costumes?
- The last act is in the middle of a cold, blustery day—what are people wearing?
- The play is about unrequited love, and this scene will have many complicated relationships on display—what arrangement of furniture and walls will intensify these relationships?
- This room has been turned into Constantine's study—he wants to be seen as an artist—how does that affect the décor of this room?

As you study the scene in more detail, you need to make some practical decisions, only some of which you can leave until rehearsal.

- The room has three doors—to the garden, to the dining room, and to the front hallway—where can they be placed to allow for flow?
- Are there enough places to move in the scene? Remember, at one point, nine characters are on stage. There needs to be a place for Constantine to write, for Sorin to sleep, and for several people to play a bingo sort of game
- Should there be enough places to sit for all nine folks?

One of the analysis tools I love to use during the design process is the moment chain. As you'll remember from Chapter 2, the moment chain comprises the twenty-four most important events in the play. Before final decisions are made, check your moment chain against the ground plans, lighting ideas, and what you know about sound and costumes.

- Now that you've had discussions with your designers, are these still the most important moment in the show? Or has your thinking shifted?
- Imagine each moment on your potential set—is there a place that makes sense for each one?

- Think about what you've discussed so far in terms of costume, sound, and lights—will you have the tools to detonate these moments?
- Are there places you plan to wow the audience with design choices that are perhaps not the most important moments? Are you being led astray from the story by spectacle?

During a design process it's easy to get excited about certain scenes in the show that might be fun to make into a spectacle. But ask yourself if these are the moments that audiences should be focusing on. I remember working on *She Kills Monsters* and being led astray by the many fight scenes. While they were spectacular, I wonder if the story of the two sisters would have affected the audience more if we pulled back on some of the razzle dazzle.

SORTING THROUGH PRACTICAL DECISIONS

Directors must prioritize how to spend money on their shows. It doesn't matter what size show you are working on; no budget is unlimited. Even on professional shows, typically the first draft of set and costumes designs come in well over budget.

At first, the production manager, set designer, and technical director will put their heads together and look for ways to cut costs. Perhaps the theatre company has some flats or platforms or other scenery in stock, or in storage, and with slight alterations to the design, these can be used to bring costs down. Or perhaps they can source a cheaper material than the designer had originally envisioned. Hopefully the theatre company has some costume stock that can be used.

At a certain point, the technical team makes as many invisible changes to the set as possible and turns to the director. It's not the director's job to know how sets are built or figure out ways to cut costs. The director's job is to ask for a list of things that might be changed or cut and then help set a list of priorities. If you're in this position, once again, think about story. What must you have to tell the story effectively and what would be nice to have, but is really icing on a cake?

No matter what budget you start with or what level of support, I encourage you to engage in a design process. If all you are doing is choosing and arranging chairs, you still need to figure out the color of the chairs and how to place them. If you have fifty dollars to spend, you need to decide how to spend each penny. The more discussions you have with other people about the physical aspects of the show, the more exciting decisions you make as a group. The more choices you make, the clearer you become about the production.

SUMMARY

In this chapter we have introduced key ideas around designing the world of the play:

* Assembling a design team
* Leading design meetings
    * Developing and expressing a point of view
    * Evaluating concepts
    * Working towards a final design

FURTHER READING

I recommend two non-theatre books about leadership in preparing to run collaborative design meetings. *Start With Why* by Simon Sinek suggests that great leadership comes from developing a compelling "why" for a project and finding people who share your why. *Emergent Strategy* by adrienne maree brown, suggests ways to lead groups that dismantle hierarchy and seek to embrace change and disorder.

HELPFUL WEBSITES

www.howlround.com is a free and open website devoted to essays about theatrical practices and they have content from actors, directors, dramaturgs, and designers about the field.

www.tcg.org is the website of Theatre Communications Group, which exists to strengthen all the professional non-profit theatres in the country.

4

CASTING

Auditions exhilarate and educate directors.

Hearing the play out loud makes the show feel real. Watching different people inhabit the characters teaches you more about the play than hours of reading the script. Auditions bridge the gap between reading and thinking about the play and putting it into action. After choosing costumes and set pieces, now you make crucial decisions about who will play which part.

Typically, the audition process will start after the design process and overlap. As you finalize designs, you put the finishing touches on your cast list.

In this process you'll:

- Prepare for auditions
  - Create character descriptions
  - Compile and contact potential actors
  - Pull sides for actors to read
- Auditions actors
- Make the final cast list

At each decision point the play becomes more concrete. You may hear the phrase that "casting is 70% of directing." Human interactions and relationships form the center of your play. Once you've cast someone in a role, you've decided a certain pathway. In rehearsal

DOI: 10.4324/9781003016922-4

you will make many choices and help shape performances, but the essence of the person you've cast will come through.

CREATING CHARACTER DESCRIPTIONS

Take your first step to prepare for auditions by writing a break-down: for each character create a short paragraph outlining what you're looking for in an actor. These should be descriptive enough that they help organize the pool of actors, but open enough that you can be surprised by someone about whom you weren't thinking. In a professional situation, these paragraphs would go out to agents, people who represent actors. How do you write these breakdowns?

In his seminal book, *Backwards and Forwards*, David Ball introduces the idea of character bones. A script only gives you the skeleton of the role—actors will provide the muscle and sinew. First, compile the basics of who the person is: age, gender, profession, class. Next, look at what they do—this is how we know people—by their actions. The basic bones for Walter Lee in *A Raisin in the Sun* are:

- Black man
- Mid 30s in 1950s—so born in the 1920s
- Lived entire life in Chicago
- Married with one ten-year-old son
- Has been employed as a chauffeur for many years
- Has one younger sister and lives with his mother

If we think back to chapter two and the discussion of stage directions, notice I avoid some of the more vivid descriptions from the stage directions. I don't list that he is a "lean intense young man" or that "in his voice there is a quality of indictment." Instead, I examine his major actions. What does he do?

- Tries to convince family to give him insurance money to invest in a liquor store
- Dreams about a more successful future
- Puts his trust in a friend to use money to pay off a licensing official

- Deceives family by taking some of Beneatha's college fund
- Tells family he will take the money from the white organization in Clybourn Park
- Changes his mind and rejects offer of money
- Leads the charge in the move to new house

At this point you know some things about the actor who will play Walter Lee, but many things are up for consideration. What does the actor look like or sound like? Is he charming or a bit combative? Does he feel like a man or a boy? A father or a son? What forms his core personality? Your choices about who plays Walter determine how the audience views him.

At this point I ask myself—what is the one thing this character needs to have that you cannot teach? In a short rehearsal period, you'll be able to work on many things—characterization, staging, emotional response—but someone's essence as a person still shines through. If you're casting a part that is primarily comedic—find someone funny. If you need someone who takes high status—search for a person who can hold the center of attention. If I was advising a directing student working on *Raisin*, I might suggest that the one thing you can't teach Walter is that he's a frustrated leader. Walter should be at the head of a company, but can't find a way in. Here's a potential breakdown for Walter Lee and a few other characters:

Walter Lee: Black, male, mid-thirties. A husband, father, and oldest son—recently lost his father. Works as a chauffeur but dreams of more. Willing to cut some corners to chase his dreams. Decent at his core. A frustrated leader. In another circumstance, would likely be running his own business.

Beneatha: Black, female, mid-20s. Daughter and younger sister. Studying to be a doctor, almost unheard of for a Black woman. An atheist, bucking the trend of her family and community. Striving for more, struggling between her own desires and what her family needs.

Ruth: Black, Female, early 30s. Mother, sister-in-law, daughter in law. Works as a domestic for a rich white family, and as a 1950s mother runs the household, cooking and cleaning. She often acts as a peacemaker and a pragmatist.

You'll note these breakdowns avoid physical details such as height, weight, or particulars of what characters look like. This encourages a casting director to think broadly about these characters and not jump to stereotypes. While Walter Lee is the male lead of the show, and may typically be cast with a "leading man type." What does that mean exactly? What does a leader look like? Do they have to be fit and muscular? Tall and lean? Better to focus on ability and essence rather than superficial details.

TRY THIS: WRITE CHARACTER BREAKDOWNS

- For each character write a short paragraph:
  - What are the basics about age, race, ethnicity, gender, role?
  - What can't you teach about the character?
  - What big action does the character perform in the play?

What did you learn about your play by being precise about the characters? Who do you imagine in these roles now?

COMPILING LISTS OF ACTORS

Now that you have an idea of who you are looking for, compile lists of actors who might fit each part. At this point a director works by themselves, with an assistant, with an academic advisor, or with a professional casting director. If you are working in an academic setting, try to find someone who knows the acting company to discuss these lists—this conversation can help you refine your thinking about the characters.

When a casting director presents a line-up, they are responding to your vision for the show, but also putting in their own ideas about who might play the character. Perhaps there is an actor you've never heard of; the casting director can explain why they added them to the mix. The most interesting and revealing conversations arise when your lists clash. Explaining why you don't think someone is right for a role helps you more clearly understand the character.

Say you are casting the role of Nina from *The Seagull* and the casting director puts someone on the list that you think isn't quite right. You could imagine a conversation like this:

CD: Oh, she just seems like a naïve, sweet girl. I saw her in something where she really was able to be guileless and simple.

D: Oh! That's not what I was thinking at all for Nina. Yes, she's inexperienced, but look at what she does in the play. She's ambitious, she's even a bit cutthroat. I think we need to see stronger women in that part.

At this point you could cut the person from the list, or perhaps you could decide to see them anyway. Maybe they have those qualities and abilities but haven't been able to show them off.

If you can't work with a casting director—I encourage you to discuss your ideas with someone. Maybe you can bring aboard an assistant director or perhaps a dramaturg. If you have an academic advisor, talk through potential actors with them. Being able to defend your hunches sharpens your understanding of the play.

In the second chapter we spoke about the need for a director to serve as their own literary manager of sorts, constantly on the search for new plays to read. In the same way, directors should have a clear idea of the acting community. If you're a student, be sure to attend as many shows as possible to see actors in action. If you're starting out in the professional world—seek out productions in a variety of venues. You want to have a sense of the acting pool so you can make great suggestions when it comes time to create lists for auditions.

PULLING AUDITION SIDES

The next step in the audition process is pulling auditions sides for each character. Sides are short scenes or portions of scenes you'll ask actors to prepare. Many directors I interviewed saw choosing sides as a crucial step in the process. They picked scenes that revealed character and made demands of the actors. For a small character you might only choose one side, and for a leading character you might choose as many as four. I like to choose two sides for each character. I select two contrasting scenes so we can see the actor work a comedic or gentle bit and a tough or dramatic moment. When choosing, I look for scenes that ask for the quality you cannot teach and reveal the character breakdown.

When choosing sides, find something where the character makes a big decision or encounters a dramatic event. You want to see if the actor can handle change in a scene. You probably don't want to choose the most dramatic scene in the play, such as the climax. Actors won't really be able to pull off a scene like that without the entire play behind them. Aside from character, you might also consider what they do in the play. Do they have a bunch of monologues? Make sure to pull one to see if your actor can activate a lot of text. How about fast back and forth comedic dialogue? Do they need to dominate scenes or be a quiet presence in the background?

In terms of length, if you're working with a manuscript, a typed-out script, your sides don't need to be longer than two pages. If you're working with a printed script from the rights agency, you may only need one page; something that runs about three minutes. Remember you want the actors to fully prepare the sides, and you want time to work with the material in auditions. You will watch this side over and over in auditions, so pick a scene you like!

If I was pulling sides for Constantine in *The Seagull*, I would choose the scene with his mother in Act Three as the first side. He asks his mother to change his bandage, recalling happier times when they lived together. After a moment's peace, Constantine asks his mother to leave her boyfriend and a fight erupts.

This scene cuts to the core of Constantine's essence. He deeply needs his mother's affection, starts out loving and kind, and ends with vitriol and rage. It shows off his insecurity as an artist and highlights his need for validation. As a second side, I might choose the long story he tells about Nina in the fourth act. Constantine goes through a huge change in the two years between acts—can the actor embody that transformation? Also, he needs to activate a huge amount of text and be able to tell a great story.

TRY THIS: PULL AUDITIONS SIDES FOR A PLAY

- Pick one or two characters from a play.
- What do you need to see an actor do to know if they are right for the part?
- Choose two contrasting sides of a few pages each.

What did you learn about these characters by asking yourself to pull sides? What did it feel like to choose one scene as opposed to another? What have you learned about the play by choosing these sides?

RECRUITING ACTORS AND SETTING UP AUDITIONS

You might be in a situation where you are part of a formal audition process, one that's handled by the theatre department or theatre company. Make sure you understand what is expected of you and when you need to make deadlines. Verify whether you have unlimited time to see actors, or if you'll need to work on a short timeframe.

On the other hand, you may need to recruit interested actors to audition for your play. You may need to put up posters around your school or post messages on social media to generate interest in your production. Try to be encouraging, succinct, and clear with these audition notices:

- What is the play?
- Why is it exciting?
- When does it perform?
- When are auditions?
- What do people need to prepare?
- What experience or talents are necessary?

Now you can decide how you want to see auditions. Do you want to have everyone interested come in and do a short monologue and then you'll decide who to call back for certain roles? Do you want to have short conversations with everyone to gauge their interest and then guide them toward certain characters? Do you want people to self-select sides and then come to an audition period?

If possible, it's best for you and for all the people involved if you set up some sort of schedule, so that no one's time is wasted. Be clear about what you want to see, what you're expecting, and then coordinate a time and a place.

At this session, be sure to have each actor fill out an audition form that lists their experience, any potential conflicts with the rehearsal period, and their contact information. Also make sure you let everyone know when you'll be making your decisions and how they will find out if they were cast or not.

WORKING WITH ACTORS IN THE AUDITION ROOM

Finally, you're working with actors in person.

Remember that for an actor, an audition can be a nerve-wracking process. They may have their hopes set on a part, they could be doubting themselves, maybe they are intimidated by you (yes you!), or the situation. If an actor is scared, you may not experience their best performance, so do what you can to set them at ease.

A typical audition session with an actor reading a side might go like this:

- Actor enters and is greeted by the director and introduced to anyone else who might be in room (assistants, dramaturgs, readers)
- Actor is asked which side they'd like to do first and if they have any questions
- Actor does the audition one time through without stopping
- The director and actor speak for a moment, and the director gives an adjustment—a simple bit of direction to do the scene differently
- The actor does the side one time through again
- If time allows and the director wants to give another adjustment, they do
- If time allows, they repeat the process for a second side
- Actor is dismissed

I like to hold auditions in this manner because it respects the actor's process and allows them the opportunity to show off their first take on the scene. It also allows the director to see if the actor is easy to work with, and if they can take adjustments. An adjustment is simply any direction given to an actor asking them to do the scene differently.

As you watch the actor do their first take on a scene, really try to see what's in front of you. Try to avoid viewing the scene through the lens of some "perfect version" in your head, but instead observe the actors. In this first round, look out for the following:

- Are you drawn to them?
- Are they prepared?
- Are they listening to their partner?
- Do they change from the beginning of the scene to the end?
- Did they make any surprising choices?

After you watch this first round, I encourage you to have a short conversation with the actor. Try leading with questions. What do they think this scene is about? What is their relationship with the partner? What do they want in the scene? If they made a surprising choice, you might ask about it. What led them to that choice?

After this conversation—give some sort of adjustment and keep your direction simple. Try to lead the actor to a performance that makes the scene more dynamic and interesting. I use many ideas from *Audition* by Michael Shurtleff to guide my work with actors. In this book, Shurtleff outlines twelve guideposts for actors in preparing for auditions. I tend to focus on his first three: relationship, fighting for, and moment before.

Imagine I'm auditioning the role of Constantine and I've just watched an actor do the fight scene with his mother from Act Three. I can imagine using these three guideposts to direct the actor. I love to ask a lot of questions, then give a simple task.

- Relationship
    - What is your relationship with your mother like in general? What's it like right now? Why are you in conflict with her? Why do you love her? What does it matter to you if she listens to you right now?

- • If the actor had shown only scorn for his mother,
     I might suggest they lean into their love for their
     mother.
- Fighting For
  - • What do you want in this moment from your mother?
       What do you need from her in this scene? Do you think
       you can get that right now?
  - • If the actor said they wanted comfort, I might suggest they
       really fight for that comfort from their mother. (Fighting
       for is another way to define action or what the character
       wants from their partner.)
- Moment Before
  - • What happened just before the scene began? Where are you
       coming from? How does that affect the top of the scene?
    - • In this case, we know that Constantine rushed in to
         help his uncle who was having some sort of fainting
         spell. He hadn't planned to talk to his mother or ask
         her to change his bandage. It's a spur of the moment
         idea—how does that change the attack at the top?

To recap: an actor comes in, I greet them, let them do the side one
time with no direction and then have a conversation about relationship, fighting for, and the moment before the scene begins. If I think
that's enough direction, I might just let them do the scene again and
then move on. If I have more time, or I want to see the actor work
again, I might turn to some of Shurtleff's other guideposts.

I encourage you to look over all twelve guideposts which include
discovery, importance, humor, competition, and secrets. Perhaps on a
third take on the scene, I might ask them to focus on making discoveries in the moment or seeking out the humor in the scene. It all depends
on their first take and my hunch on how to improve the scene.

CASTING THE PLAY

You're finally ready to create a cast list!

If you're lucky, you'll have clear first choices for every part, you'll
make your offers, and everyone accepts. Typically, the process takes a
bit more deliberation, as you need to make choices between actors.
I encourage you to find a partner and discuss your casting ideas. This

should be someone you completely trust, to give you honest feedback, and keep your conversations private and confidential!

In the professional world you might have discussions with the artistic director and the casting director and other artistic staff. In your case, can you bring on an assistant director? Or could you talk about casting with your dramaturg or your design team? Having a discussion is often the best way to find clarity around a decision.

As you create your cast list, think about the story you are telling. If I was casting *The Seagull*, I could imagine facing a choice between two possible Nina's. Perhaps one Nina perfectly captures her innocence, naivete and fresh attitude towards the world, and would need to work to capture the grim and jaded last scene of the play. If the other actor felt just right for the last scene, but perhaps was a stretch for the first few acts, I have a choice. In one version of the story Nina hides her jaded view of the world by projecting innocence, and in the other tragic events snuff out her sunny disposition.

If you can, take a few days to think about the casting, reading over your play with different actors in mind. How would this scene play with these two actors? What if I substituted these two? Go back to your analysis of the play—which group of actors will help connect the audience to your point of view on the script?

TRY THIS: FANTASY CASTING

- Pick a play that you know and love.
- Put together a short list of famous actors to play the lead parts, maybe even pull their photographs.
- Read through a key scene or two, trying out different actors in your mind.

Could you imagine the actors in those parts? How did one person read the scene differently from another? How was the story different depending on who played the parts?

CASTING IN AN ACADEMIC ENVIRONMENT

If you're casting at the college or high school level, you may run into special situations. These rarified casting situations provide great training for working on plays outside of school.

In one version of academic casting, you may have no designated actors at your disposal. Perhaps you just need to recruit whoever you can find to fill your cast. Great! Practice communicating your vision and recruiting talented people to your projects. In the professional world, people don't always take every project that comes their way. Money is a motivating factor, but only up to a certain point. For an actor to commit themselves to at least two or three months of work, they need to believe in the project, have faith they will be treated well, and feel confident in their ability to succeed in the part.

In another version of casting in a school setting, several shows audition at the same time, and actors must be distributed among several casts. In the professional world you also compete against other projects. You just might not know what the projects are, and you won't be competing directly, but you still won't always get the actors you want the most. Developing a sense of flexibility and imagination around casting will serve you well in the long run.

If you are casting in a version where several directors come together and need to compromise to figure out where each actor will be placed, come prepared with many options. You'll want to have several people in your mind for every part in your show, especially for the smaller parts. And you'll need to clearly articulate why you want certain people and what the role entails. Being able to publicly explain the demands of a role and the talent of a certain actor is a great skill to develop.

SUMMARY

In this chapter we have introduced ideas around Casting:

- Developing Character Breakdowns
- Pulling Auditions Sides from the Play
- Running Effective Auditions

FURTHER READING

Audition: Everything an Actor Needs to Know to Get the Part by Michael Shurtleff and *Auditioning: An Actor Friendly Guide* by Joanna Merlin are two excellent guides to the auditioning process from the actor's perspective, but will give insights for directors as well. *Tips: Ideas for Actors* by Jon Jory has excellent ideas for all aspects of directing, but his acting coaching and casting tips are especially handy for auditions.

HELPFUL WEBSITES

There are several places that audition notices are posted, and viewing these will give you some examples of character breakdowns:

www.backstage.com
www.theatreinchicago.com
www.actorsaccess.com.

5

REHEARSING

Rachel Chavkin, Tony Award winning director of *Hadestown*, told me during an interview that great rehearsals involve making choices. The more choices made the better. A scene doesn't mean anything to Chavkin until she and her collaborators make it mean something: Does the scene start with people standing or sitting? Close or far apart? Do these people love each other? Hate each other? Chavkin strives for specificity in rehearsal by changing her mind to find better solutions to scenes. She has a pithy equation for how rehearsal works: the amount of time you have in rehearsal equals the number of choices you'll be able to make. Since you can't make a better choice until you make a first choice: start making decisions early.

By the first rehearsal you made some key choices, including a point of view about the story, and how you want to impact the audience. With your designers you created a physical world. You chose who will be in the play, and in doing so made decisions about the story.

During rehearsal, you guide your actors to make choices about staging, character development, emotional impact, and specificity of moments. You figure out how the play moves, how one scene flows into the next, and the rhythm of certain sections versus others. Once technical rehearsals begin the director leads collaborations with stage managers, designers, and actors to incorporate all the design elements.

DOI: 10.4324/9781003016922-5

But how do you structure this movement from page to stage? From idea to flesh? From general to specific?

TRY THIS: WHAT CHOICES ARE THERE TO MAKE?

- Look at the first scene of a play, read it over a few times.
- What choices will you need to make when you work on it?
- Try to list as many choices as possible that are specific to the scene itself.

We've talked about establishing given circumstances for a scene; how do you understand a scene differently by looking from the other side? Were you surprised at how many choices a scene offers? What kinds of choices excite you the most to explore?

CREATING A REHEARSAL SCHEDULE

Your theatre company or department typically sets a schedule for when rehearsal starts, how many hours per day you can work, and how many days a week. They determine how long you have in the rehearsal studio, how much time for tech, and when audiences arrive. But within this skeleton, directors determine how best to use their time. The director and the stage manager work closely in this process, learning together the rhythms of the production.

When I first started directing plays I scheduled every day down to the minute, allotting the same amount of time for each scene, scheduling every day out a month in advance. I learned that a rigid schedule didn't allow for discovery, and it assumed every scene needed the same amount of time. Now I work with flexibility, setting schedules week by week as I discover how the play works. I find that I never know which scene will flow on the first try, and which ones still confound us after several attempts.

At a university, you might have five days a week of four-hour rehearsal for five weeks, then a week of tech, followed by a couple of previews and then opening. American professional theatres often compress rehearsals: seven hours a day, six days a week, for only two and a half weeks of rehearsal, followed by one weekend of tech, a few previews, then opening. See Appendix 5 for a model rehearsal schedule.

As I set a schedule, I think about a series of tasks or activities and ask how much time I think each one will take.

- First Rehearsal
- Table Work/World Building
- Staging
- Detailed Scene Work
- Run-throughs
- Technical Rehearsals

Each of these phases offers specific pleasures for a director. At the first rehearsal you kick off the journey with the entire team after months of preparation. When you read the play at the table or conduct world building physical exercises, you lead an exploration of the universe of the play. Staging requires clear eyes from a director to turn ideas into flesh. When you dig into detailed scene work you uncover layers of meaning and depths of character work. With run-throughs directors see what they've created and assess next steps. In technical rehearsals you lead your entire time to bring all the elements together: acting, sets, lights, costumes, sound.

I divided this chapter into different sections but know that lines often blur when you are working. As you work deeply on scene work you continue to refine your staging and examine the text. During the initial staging of the play, you build your world, as well as think about technical elements. On the first day of rehearsal, you examine the text with your entire team.

Let's examine each of these phases in turn—starting with the exciting first day.

KICKING OFF THE FIRST REHEARSAL

A first rehearsal bursts with excitement.

Anticipation builds for months—sometimes even years—for the kickoff of work with the actors. As the director, you lead the event—what tone will you set for this next phase of discovery?

For a professional theater a common schedule for the first day might look like this:

- A meet and greet for the entire company and the staff of the theatre
- A first speech by the director
- Presentations by the designers
  - Set model
  - Costume sketches
  - Lighting renderings
  - Sound and Music samples
- A first read through of the play
- A discussion of the themes and discoveries

These first hours of rehearsal set the tone for discovery in the weeks to come—how do you want to lead this group?

CRAFTING A FIRST DAY SPEECH

After introductions, everyone will likely turn to you, the director. Why are we here? What can we expect? Why are we doing this play?

When I'm working with MFA directors, I ask them to write several drafts of first day speeches—each time pushing them to clarify their language and ideas. I encourage directors to sharpen their point of view—how do they understand the story of the play?

Imagine that everything that happens in a play is spread out on the table like metal shavings. A directorial point of view works like a magical magnet—only lifting some of the shavings—crafting a piece of art that is specific to each director.

As you head towards first rehearsal write a few drafts of opening remarks. Read them to a trusted friend or a teacher. Focus on accomplishing the following:

- Tell your version of the story of the play
  - The plot of the play contains everything that happens in the script. The story is an edited version of what happens, focusing on the events and moments that align with your interests. Can you tell a compelling story in about five sentences that grasps the heart of the play?

- Share why you chose the play
  - Think back to your first read of the script—you connected in a visceral way. Only you have this specific reaction, so be sure to share this with your collaborators.
- Define a goal
  - How will you know if you've triumphed as a group of collaborators? Is your goal to make people laugh? To disrupt their belief system? To move them to tears?
- Categorize the kind of play you're tackling
  - Not every play is alike, nor do they work the same way. Are you working on a comedy? What kind? A satire? A farce? Are you collaborating on a tragedy? A classic tragedy or something with a modern twist?
- Simply declare what the play is about
  - Directors need to hone their ability to boil something complex down to one simple sentence or sentiment. A short phrase orients actors and other collaborators, giving them a clear direction to head.

Some directors write out their speech, craft it into a sort of manifesto and read it out loud. Others memorize their remarks. I read the speech a few times and then write an outline. On the first day I improvise my language around my main points, connecting with the room and inspiring people around our collective vision.

TRY THIS: WRITE A FIRST DAY ADDRESS

- Go back to your analysis and read it over.
- Home in on your point of view.
- Write a first day address telling the story and communicating what the play is about.
- Read this to a teacher, friend, or fellow student—what notes do they have?

What did you learn about your play by trying to communicate your point of view in a short address? What kind of speaker are you? How do you want to get your ideas across?

SHOWCASING DESIGNS

After you give your speech, encourage your designers to show the cast the research they used to inspire their work. These research images will communicate with your cast on a level your words may not. Hearing potential music or sound cues can help actors understand the tone and mood of the entire play or certain scenes.

As your designers present their work, look for spots to fill in inspiration, or pose challenges and questions to the cast. As the set designer shows off the model, actors will get excited about where they will get to play for the next few weeks. You may point out where certain scenes might work best and challenge them to think about how they will use the set. When the lighting designer shows off renderings, you might speak about tone or mood.

The costume designer's presentation often generates the most excitement in the room. You and the designer discussed how a character moves, interacts, and shows themselves to the world. The actor read the script and had their own insights. Where do these visions overlap? Where do they diverge? Will there be opportunities for the actor to speak with the costumer and collaborate during fittings?

Even in these first interactions, look for ways to inspire collaboration, clarify point of view, and build trust in the room. You've created an imaginary world with designers, now it's time for the actors to inhabit this universe and flesh out your creations. Can you start dialogues across disciplines? Can costume designers begin to collaborate with actors? Is there a safe opening for an actor to ask questions about the set design?

BUILDING THE WORLD IN REHEARSAL

Every play you work on is different. Let's look at two famous Shakespeare plays.

The play *Hamlet* takes place in a series of rooms in a castle in Denmark, while *A Midsummer Night's Dream* takes place mostly in a forest. In *Hamlet* royalty engage in domestic intrigue, while in *Midsummer*, faeries interfere with humans. In *Hamlet*, characters combat through political arguments, subterfuge, and sword fights. In *Midsummer*, characters interact through word play, romantic chases, and mischief. If you're working on each of these plays, they should feel different, look different, and play different.

How do you create a fictional world in rehearsal?

Part of the world is physical; the way time and space work on people and the sounds of the world. How people dress, move, and interact with each other creates mood, tone, and feelings. The type of language people use determines how people interact.

Some directors will jump straight into staging and working on scenes early in the rehearsal, but others like to do preparatory work of group world building. How do you build a universe? Let's look at three different ideas of how to collectively figure out your play before you start staging scenes.

- Examining language and events reading around a table
- Delving into dramaturgy and research
- Building shared vocabulary through games and movement

PARSING THE SCRIPT AT THE TABLE

Table work involves actors, directors, dramaturgs, and assistants sitting around a table reading and discussing the play.

What are the main purposes of table work? To allow actors to gain an understanding of the script before being asked to jump on their feet and act. The director hears the play out loud and can start to flesh out ideas they developed in analysis. Start at the beginning, read a section, stop, and ask questions. Almost any question will help further understanding, but a few simple one's to start are:

- Who's in this scene? How do they know each other?
- What's just happened before this scene?
- What's happening in the scene?
- How is this scene different from the last one we read?
- What is the most important event that happens in this scene?
- Why does that character say that?

You can't ask all these questions about every line in the play; follow your instincts and interests. Also, don't feel you have to answer every question; leave some for actors to think about on their own or work out when you begin staging.

How much should you read before stopping to discuss? You might try reading every French scene individually. In longer French scenes you might read up until each dramatic event. As you remember, a dramatic event is a decision or turning point that affects every character on stage. By asking the question—*why did this event happen?*—you start to help develop character and point of view. You could also ask—*what would happen if this event didn't occur?* What other directions could the play take? How does this decision forward the action of the play?

If you are lucky enough to work with a dramaturg, this is a moment for them to shine. Any time the actors read a word or come across a term they don't understand, your dramaturg can probably answer their question, or better yet, point them towards some research opportunities. If you were discussing *A Raisin in the Sun*, the dramaturg should be ready to talk about red-lining, white flight, the economic situation for Blacks in Chicago in the late 1940s, the life of Lorraine Hansberry, and so on. Hopefully the actors will ask questions that you haven't even thought of, sending the dramaturg back to their research.

IMMERSING THE ACTORS IN DRAMATURGICAL RESEARCH

A few months before he starts rehearsal, Mark Wing-Davey, Professor of Acting at New York University, contacts the cast with research assignments. He asks each actor to come to the first week of rehearsal ready to give a ten-minute report or demonstration on some topic related to the play. I assistant-directed for Wing-Davey on the world premiere of *36 Views*, by Naomi Iizuka, at Berkeley Repertory Theatre in California in 2001. The play centered around intrigue within the Asian art world, so he asked me to give a report on the history of Japanese art. Others gave reports on tea ceremonies, ancient Japanese poetry, and the business of selling artifacts. These reports involve the actors in creating the world of the play and insure information comes from all corners of the room.

Wing-Davey encourages imaginative and physical reports. In one rehearsal an actor playing a fishmonger demonstrated how to fully gut, scale, and clean a fish. In another a group of actors recreated a religious ceremony with the rest of the cast.

If you were directing *The Seagull*, you could imagine a demonstration of theatrical styles from the period, a lecture on Anton

Chekhov's life and work, a sharing of traditional Russian food and drink, and an examination of a stuffed seagull. For *A Raisin in the Sun*, you might pore over maps of neighborhoods in Chicago, live a day in the life of a chauffeur, learn a traditional Nigerian dance, and listen to music that would have played at the Green Mill jazz club.

MOVING AND PLAYING TO CREATE A SHARED VOCABULARY

Some directors read and re-read the play at the table, explore the dramaturgy and research, and then jump on their feet to stage the play. Other directors teach their cast about the script through movement and play. Here's three examples.

When Kim Rubinstein was directing *A Raisin in the Sun* with her students at University of California San Diego, she wanted to make sure the apartment felt truly lived in. She held movement exercises where the actors walked around the set of the apartment in character. They could go anywhere on the set with the goal of understanding their movement habits. Where do they go in the small space to not bother anyone or to have privacy? Where do they gather for celebrations?

When West End director Robert Icke started working on his adaptation of *Mary Stuart* for The Almeida Theatre in London, he noticed his actors couldn't embody the complex social interactions around royalty. *Mary Stuart* follows the historical feud between Queen Elizabeth I and her cousin, Mary, Queen of Scots. Icke found that the Queens didn't command the respect they needed, nor did their retinue understand the social dynamics. He created "The Queen's Game"—actors were divided into teams, each with a Queen, and they were sent out into the neighborhood around the theatre. They were supposed to get a photograph of the opposing team's Queen and bring it back. Immediately the actors leapt into motion, running out to accomplish the task. Reporting back later the Queens noted their discomfort having so much responsibility and their team noted how aggressively they jockeyed for power.

When Anne Bogart works on a play with her SITI Company, they start every rehearsal with Viewpoints improvisation. As outlined in

Chapter 1, the Viewpoints training method develops actors' physicality and kinesthetic connections. Ensembles develop their sense of space, timing, shape, architecture, and other Viewpoints. Bogart's actors improvise together to wake up their bodies and create non-verbal connections as an ensemble. Sometimes they will ask a question that relates to the scenes they will work on that day before they improvise. They might explore status or longing in their improvisations, working on the play obliquely.

These three ideas are just a few examples of methods directors use to build worlds through play, improvisation, and movement. Maybe you want to do some of the composition work explained in Chapter 1. Your cast might benefit from recreating scenes from famous paintings or movies that feel connected to your project. Perhaps you want to create your own game designed around your project and ensemble.

What kind of director are you? Do you think you'd enjoy running physical improvisations? Or would you rather read the play and discuss around a table? Do you think you'll change your process depending on the kind of script you're working on?

Once you've started to build a shared vocabulary with your cast, now you can jump into the pleasures of staging. You can finally see your play in action up on its feet.

TRY THIS: IMAGINE A WORLD BUILDING SESSION

- Look over a favorite play or one you're about to direct.
- Think about the challenges the script presents. Is the language complicated? Is the world full of movement? Is it set in a period from the past?
- Think about what experiences might help actors dive into the world.
- Sketch out a week of exercises, text work, and ensemble building work.

What did you learn about your play just from this mental exercise? What makes your play different? How might you unlock the potential for your actors?

CRAFTING THE BLOCKING

The term blocking comes from the 19th century tradition of directors using colored blocks to stand in for actors and pre-plan staging. Directors spent months with a model of the set, trying out different ideas for where characters entered, how they moved about the stage, and what direction they exited. As they made discoveries, they would mark down the staging in their scripts. During rehearsals they moved their actors around the stage just as they had manipulated the wooden blocks.

In his book *The Empty Space*, Peter Brook tells the story of how he abandoned this type of directing. In 1946, when he was only twenty-one, Brook was hired by the Royal Shakespeare Company to direct *Love's Labor's Lost*. The night before the first rehearsal he practiced with little figures, prepping himself to stage the first entrance. He walked in with an impressively fat prompt book. When he came to rehearse with the actual people, his very first move didn't go according to plan. The actors didn't move like his figures the night before. He hesitated for a moment, considering drilling his cast until they executed his ideas correctly, and then abandoned his plan. Brook decided to instead create his staging organically in collaboration with his actors.

How will you stage scenes? From a preset plan? Will you follow your actors' instincts? Some combination of the two? To start figuring out your personal style, begin with the purpose of blocking: to create a repeatable pattern of movement and actions on stage that will:

- Tell the story of the scene physically
- Capture the eye and delight the audience's sense of beauty
- Communicate relationships between characters non-verbally including their level of intimacy and relative status
- Draw focus to the area of the stage that's most important
- Allow the actors to live in the scene night to night

In this book I discuss staging first and then delving into detailed scene work. These tasks naturally overlap; as you learn more about the scene you change your staging, and the best staging uncovers meaning. But I separate them so we can focus first on creating a skeleton of sorts, and then adding in the muscle and heart. We will sketch physically, and then add detail later.

In this rehearsal process you've had a first day that kicked off the proceedings then spent some time either at the table or playing games to create the world of the play. What do you do next? I like to start with a surprise run-through.

RUNNING WITHOUT BLOCKING

Moving from world building to staging can sometimes feel awkward. If you spent your time sitting and reading, actors hesitate to jump on their feet to work. If you played games, the structure of scenes and dialogue might stifle impulses.

I like to subvert these problems with a surprise run-through.

My world building sessions typically last a few days to a week. I use table work to clarify relationships, the major events of the scene, and basic given circumstances. We pepper in Viewpoints work or other physical games. When we finish the last bit of table work, I make an announcement: we're running the play on its feet from beginning to end.

This typically shocks people, and I see actors processing. Some can't wait to play, others seem less secure, and a few check to see if I'm joking.

I set out ground rules:

- If there is any intimacy or violence, they need to mark it. Perhaps they could just hug or touch someone on the shoulder.
- Beyond that, any choice is valid, there are no wrong choices because we've made no staging yet!
- They can use whatever they find in the room, or they can mime their props.
- They should just enter where they want to and play the scene where it makes sense to them.
- They can't discuss things ahead of time, or talk about how they will do something, they can only say the lines of the play.
- Have fun!

When I'm watching this first run, I don't take too many notes but instead let the play wash over me like an audience member. Afterward I see what I remember: Where did people naturally gravitate to? What parts of the stage did actors ignore? What scenes just clicked right away and what parts felt muddy? Did the actors create any transitions that you hadn't expected? Did they solve any moments you were confused about?

After it's over I circle up and start a tradition: the check in. We go around the circle and each actor gives a quick report. What did you learn? What surprised you? During this check in you learn who feels confident about their work and who's confused. Often actors voice the same questions and concerns that occurred to you. Share what you learned about the piece and what questions arose.

Now that you've seen the entire play on its feet, I encourage you to take about a week and create your first pass of the staging of the play.

CREATING A SKETCH

Creating a sketch involves making some basic choices. Feel confident you can change your mind, but remember: you can't refine any choices unless you are bold first. Start at the beginning of the play and quickly work your way through to the end. Spend about a week on creating a physical skeleton.

What choices should you make on the first pass and what should you leave until a second pass? The metaphor of the sketch might be helpful—it's the general outline of the scene, without all the detail of the shading you'll put in later.

Some elements of a sketch you want to set on a first pass:

- Every entrance and exit
  - Where do they come from or go to?
  - What is their general speed of entrance?
  - How do they enter the space?
- Any dramatic events of the scene
  - Is there a revelation of some sort? Do you want to mark it physically?
  - Is there an important pause? Do you want to set where people are for that?
- How is the beginning of the scene different from the end?
  - Do people start intimate and end separate?
  - How have the relationships changed?

- Can you capture the essence of the story and the situation?
  - Do we know what's happening?
  - Can we easily understand what's at stake for the characters?

If there are moments of intimacy or violence in your scene, it's best to put in a place marker now. Stage the scene so the characters get close to each other but then wait until the specific intimacy or violence rehearsal to really set these moments. If the actors are comfortable, a hug could take the place of a kiss. You could have someone say punch and touch a shoulder rather than doing it.

One of the most effective ways to create a sketch for a scene: investigate the conflict.

EVERY SCENE IS A CHASE SCENE

A play is created from conflict the way a painting is created with oils and canvas.

One person wants something from someone else, the other one doesn't want to give in to their demands. Depending on the kind of play how the person tries to get what they want varies—perhaps they engage in a sword fight, or they launch into a long rhetorical monologue, or perhaps they make an emotional plea, or they never speak directly, instead talking about trivialities.

In their book *Notes on Directing*, Frank Hauser and Russel Reich summarize their views on conflict: Every scene is a chase scene.

Character A wants something from character B. Character B doesn't want to give it up. In the first scene of *A Raising in the Sun*, Walter Lee wants his wife Ruth to back his plan to finance a liquor store but she's against the notion, so Walter chases Ruth. As he attempts to win, the stronger the resistance from Ruth, the more exciting the scene.

Hauser and Reich suggest characters should physically chase each other, not just emotionally. Walter should come at, approach, and try to corner Ruth, while she retreats, escapes, and regroups. In some cases, it will make sense for this kind of movement to be large and sweeping, with a literal chase around the stage. In other cases, the chase may be more subtle, both actors sitting at a table, but one leaning forward while the other leans back.

The most exciting scenes occur when the chase switches sides. When Walter keeps haranguing his wife about the liquor store, eventually she snaps and tells him to finish his eggs. Walter stops chasing. Now Ruth is chasing him—trying to cajole him to understand her point of view, to see things from her side, and Walter evades.

When you start to create a sketch for a scene ask these questions: What is the conflict in this scene? What's at stake? Who is chasing whom?

USING THE ENTIRE STAGE

As you create your first pass sketch, think about using the entire stage.

Have you used the corners? The back wall? Does most of your play happen down center? If the stage picture doesn't change for an entire evening the audience's eyes glaze over, and their attention wanders. If you stage every scene in the same place, you're giving each scene the same value and assigning them the same meaning.

Let's first talk about an end stage or proscenium set up where the audience is on one side of the stage and actors on the other. The entire audience views the same stage picture. In this scenario a stage can be divided into six quadrants, and in the theatre, we describe these quadrants from the actors' point of view. An actor walks "down" when they approach the audience and "up" when they retreat. An actor crosses stage right when they move to their own right when facing downstage (from an audience's point of view the actor is walking to the left.)

In their comprehensive textbook, *Fundamentals of Play Directing*, Alexander Dean and Lawrence Carra describe how audiences view the stage and respond to staging. They suggest that, as a rule, Western audiences read from left to right and so find images on their left warmer and more inviting. Also, people connect easier to things that are closer to them rather than far away. Finally, objects in the center of our field of vision command more power than those on the sides.

Dean and Carra use this psychology and assign each quadrant of the stage with certain characteristics as well as ranking them from strongest to weakest in terms of how they will impact an audience.

If you're working in a three-quarter thrust staging, then some of the same rules apply. Down center commands the most power, followed by the regal up center. But because down left and up right will be different for different audience members, they won't affect people the same way.

Areas of the Proscenium Stage

Upstage Right: 5th Strongest	Upstage Center: 2nd Strongest	Upstage Left: WEAKEST
Romance	Royalty	Ghost
Illusion	Status	Unsettling
Distant	Stability	Infinity
Downstage Right: 3rd Strongest	Downstage Center: STRONGEST	Downstage Left: 4th Strongest
Intimacy	Fights	Intrigue
Monologues	Heat	Gossip
Warmth	Intense	Business

Audience

Figure 5.1

Areas of the Thrust Stage

	Upstage Corner:	Upstage Center:	Upstage Corner:	
Audience	Distance	Royalty	Distance	**Audience**
	Illusion	Status	Illusion	
	Downstage Corner:	Downstage Center:	Downstage Corner:	
	Intimacy	Fights	Intimacy	
	Intrigue	Heat	Intrigue	

Audience

Figure 5.2

When you're working through your first pass of staging, think about employing the qualities of the different parts of the stage. When do you want to use the strongest area of the stage? When do you really want something to land in the audience's lap? What scenes would benefit by being a bit farther from the audience, more distant—either up right where images feel warmer or up left, which gives off a colder vibe?

You might also try to undermine these conventions. While down right is traditionally seen as the right place to stage a soliloquy because it feels intimate and warm—perhaps you want to subvert this? Maybe you want to unsettle the audience by placing the monologue down left, or even up left? You can think of each of these first choices as an experiment, something to try out and see if it feels right or helps tell the story.

Let's check our progress in this rehearsal process. We started with a first day, kicking off the discovery period, clueing actors into our design work and our point of view. We spent some time, perhaps a week or so, building the world either through table work or movement exercises. Now we've spent another week or so creating a physical sketch of the show. You answered some of the questions about each scene and set some loose blocking. You explored the conflict of each scene and figure out basic relationships.

At this point some people will do a quick run-through just to see what they have, while others will just go back to the beginning and start adding detail. We'll go over how to use run-throughs in just a bit, but first let's dig into detailed scene work.

TRY THIS: CREATE PICTURES FOR YOUR MOMENT CHAIN

- Pull up your moment chain, or focus on say six key moments.
- Where would each moment have the most impact?
- Try out a moment in a different place on the stage? How does that affect the moment?
- Can you make little sketches of the moments?

What did you learn about your key moments by thinking about them on a stage? How did they translate from a purely intellectual idea to a physicalized one?

DELVING INTO SCENE WORK

You created a basic framework for each scene: now delve deeper. In your second and possibly third passes, rigorously explore character, emotion, and motivation. Start by simply running the scene and taking stock. Talk to everyone involved afterward and establish what seems to be working. What parts of the scene seem to click and feel right? I encourage you to trust your instincts and look for the positive. Praising actors from the beginning will yield results down the line.

Now, what aspect of the scene isn't working? It may be that you can tell immediately that some part of the staging feels awkward. Or perhaps an actor doesn't understand a moment and you can talk about it. But sometimes you won't know for certain what isn't working, or you can just sense that the scene hasn't reached its potential. It could be funnier, more exiting, more moving, more keenly observed, more human.

How can you help the actors find the next level of truth and drama? How can you help them get away from generally doing the scene to truly living in the moment? I encourage you to home in on the basics we learned from Stanislavski: given circumstances and action.

Who is in the scene? Who are they to each other? What do they want from each other? What has happened that affects the scene? Where are they? When does the scene take place? Why are they acting this way? Each of these questions, asked in rehearsal, will help unlock the scene in different ways and lead actors to richer, fuller performances.

Let's examine each one of these questions using one scene from *The Seagull* as an example. In the middle of Act 1, Constantine presents his play with his girlfriend, Nina, as the sole actor. His mother, Arkadina, and her famous boyfriend, Trigorin, along with his uncle and other household friends gather to watch. As the play continues, Arkadina starts to make jokes. Constantine abruptly stops the play, yells at his mother, and storms off. Let's examine how asking basic questions can deepen the work on this scene.

WHO IS IN THE SCENE?

"Who are you talking to?"

When you ask an actor about the state of their relationship you ground them in the given circumstances, help them become less self-conscious, get them on action, and provide texture to scenes. A scene where the actors have dug into their relationship fully can bristle with life and moment to moment surprises. Let's look at the key relationship in the scene between Arkadina and Constantine.

- How are you related?
  - Obviously mother and son, but what is the state of that relationship now?
- How much do you stay in contact?
  - They used to live together, but no longer. When did they see each other last?
- What's the relative status between you two? Who has power?
  - Is there a general state of status? Does that ever change? Does the power shift in this scene?
- How do you love this person?
  - What about them turns you on or warms you or makes you feel good?
- What is your conflict with them?
  - How do you wish they treated you differently?

Some directors believe that the relationship between two characters never really changes for an entire play, only the topic of conversation. In every scene they have together Constantine wants to be validated by his mother. In the first act he seeks recognition for his play, in the third act he's seeking acceptance for his opinions about her lover, and in the last act he longs for affirmation of his writing. The topic of the battle changes, but the essential conflict remains the same.

The relationship between Constantine and Arkadina drives the action of our scene, but Constantine must balance his relationship with everyone else as well. What does he think about his girlfriend as she's performing the play? Is he nervous in front of Trigorin, a famous author? Does he feel support from his uncle and perhaps judgement from the estate caretaker? How does his attitude change as he faces each character in the scene?

WHAT DO YOU WANT?

In his book *A Sense of Direction*, William Ball offers a golden key to unlock any scene: What does the character want? Ball notes that in the theatre this idea of wants or desires may be expressed in many ways. You might hear someone ask any of these questions:

- What do you want?
- What do you need?
- What are you after?
- What are you doing?
- What is your objective?
- What is your action?
- What verb are you playing?
- What are you fighting for?

Choose one of these questions that strike a chord for you and ask it often. Or perhaps you'll find that one actor responds when you ask them what they want, and another ignites when you inquire what they are fighting for. You should experiment in rehearsal with your language, looking for the questions that best arouse discoveries for your actors.

As you probe actors, be sure they want something specific from their partner, rather than something general or theoretical. If you ask Constantine what he wants in this scene, he might say he wants to feel great about his own play. These desires will turn him in on himself. What does he want from Arkadina? He wants his mother to validate his artwork and his feelings. He wants her to respect him as an equal. He wants her to act like his mother and treat him nicely.

WHAT IS AT STAKE?

When we go to a sporting event of any kind, we root for one team to win and the other to lose. If the teams are evenly matched, perhaps the score will go back and forth several times, building suspense. Who will score more points before the game is over? We're invested because we know what's at stake.

What's at stake when Constantine presents his play for his family and friends? No one has seen the play before and for him it's a huge artistic moment. It stars Nina, his one true love, and he's presenting it for his mother, her famous writer boyfriend, and all the people he loves. He's nervous about it coming off well. Immediately his mother sabotages the play by making jokes and the tension rises—the stakes are huge. He tries to calm his mother down—will he get the play back on track? And eventually the game is over—he stops the play. His mother wins and he stomps off, destroyed.

After you establish the complexity of the relationships in a scene, ask about conflict and stakes. You may find these two prompts help the scene feel exciting, dramatic, and human. But you may not. The scene may still feel off, boring, or confusing. Why? What's next? Perhaps you need to re-examine the basic facts of the scene.

WHAT ARE THE GIVEN CIRCUMSTANCES?

When we go to a sporting event, we know what's at stake because we understand the rules of the game. The regulations define how people can score points, what's allowed and not allowed, and how to win. Understanding how the game works allows us to invest.

Given circumstances serve as the equivalent of rules at a sporting match. They let us know what's allowed and not allowed, they tell us who has status, they give us back history about the characters. They help us determine what is at stake.

When you work on amassing a huge list of given circumstances during your reading phase, you learn about the rules of this fictional world. You figure out what is important, what motivates people, what hidden forces move the characters. When you prepare for scene work look through your list of given circumstances and pluck out those that affect the scene at hand.

If we're examining the moment Constantine puts on his play for his family, some of these givens are help raise the stakes:

- Constantine's mother is a famous actor, his father was a famous actor
- Constantine had to drop out of school before finishing
- Constantine has no job an no prospects
- Constantine and Nina just kissed before the play began, and he declared his love for her

All of these contribute to raising the stakes for Constantine. It matters more to him that the evening is a success because he feels it will impact the rest of his life. It may not mean anything to his mother, but for Constantine, it's life or death.

WHERE DOES THE SCENE TAKE PLACE?

In her book, *Theatre Games for Rehearsal: A Director's Handbook*, Viola Spolin outlines countless games for helping actors create a sense of truth from imaginary given circumstances. Several games center around ground plan and place. As a great lover of mime and imagination, Spolin had actors create whole spaces just with their imagination: a store, a diner, someone's home. In her exercises, actors help the audience "see" the imaginary ground plan just through their behavior.

For the scene where Constantine puts on his play we know the following:

- It's outdoors on a muggy night
- It's just turned 8:30pm and the moon is rising
- For some people this is their year-round home, others are visiting for a few days
- The estate has been altered to put up a little stage and an audience seating area

If you're watching a scene and the actors don't feel grounded in the fictional world, spend some time talking about the space. What is this space to them? What does it mean for this scene to happen here? Ask them some environmental questions. What do they see? What can they hear? What is the temperature? Can they smell anything? Ask these questions and then run the scene again, you'll find that the actors are more grounded.

WHEN DOES THE SCENE TAKE PLACE?

Anton Chekhov wrote hundreds of short stories before he started writing plays, mastering the art of economic writing. He also wrote thousands of letters to family members, friends, business associates, and others, practicing the art of observation and communicating details about his vacations, his work, or interactions with people. He brought these skills at scene setting to bear in his plays, mastering the art of using place and time. With a Chekhov play—always ask "when" the scene takes place:

- What season are we in?
- Do characters feel a time pressure of any sort? Why?
- When does the scene happen in the play?

Season: In the first scene of *The Seagull* the characters speak often about how muggy and humid it feels. In the second act characters complain about the heat—this act eventually explodes with a fight between Arkadina and Shamrayev. Perhaps the broiling sun adds to their level of irritation. Finally, in the last act everyone speaks about the howling wind, the cold, and the sense of gloom from the weather.

Time pressure: In the first act Constantine is stressed out because he needs the show to begin at a certain time to use the natural light of the moon. Nina only has thirty minutes because she must sneak home before her father and stepmother notice she's left. The entire third act is under a time pressure as we know that Arkadina and Trigorin are leaving the estate.

When in the play: Time might also refer to duration or how much time has elapsed. The first three acts of *The Seagull* all take place in just a few weeks over the summer. Without time to process events, people behave reactively and impulsively. But the fourth act happens two years later. People have had time to think about things, huge events have changed people's lives, people have gotten older.

How can you employ a sense of time into your directing? If you're watching a scene that seems to be a bit slack—ask yourself—is there a clock ticking? Would a sense of pressure up the stakes? If two characters encounter each other after a long absence, can you feel that in the way they treat each other? Or do they feel like they saw each other just five minutes ago? How long have characters known each other? How many times have they had this kind of fight?

WHY?

After establishing who is in the scene, the basic situation and the conflict, the important given circumstances, where and when the scene takes place, you can continue to ask questions to spur actors. Asking questions keeps a director curious. You can direct an entire scene just by asking a series of questions based on the progression of action:

- Why do you enter?
- Why do you speak to that person?
- Why do you bring up that topic of conversation?
- Why are you fighting?
- Why do you use that line of argument?
- Why do you give in? Why don't you give up the argument?
- Why do you leave?
- Why do you stay?

In the first act of *The Seagull*, Arkadina starts to talk during Constantine's play. Why? She doesn't have to do this; she could just watch dutifully and giver her son either compliments or criticisms after. But she chooses to make jokes. Why?

Is it because, as Treplev says earlier in the play, she's jealous of any theatre event that doesn't include her? Is it because she thought it was a joke or a bit of fun as she says after her son has run away? Was she simply trying to entertain the guests? Is she a bit drunk after dinner? Is she bored?

Only ask questions you're truly curious about. Actors can smell when you're running a test or a quiz, or merely want them to say what's in your head. Instead cultivate a level of curiosity in yourself and your cast. Think of a scene as a group project to solve—by asking "why," everyone starts to examine the characters from different angles.

WHAT IS THE KEY EVENT OF THE SCENE?

One final bit of advice about scene work: Can you identify and then delay the key event? Remember back to our work in the reading chapter where we talked about cause and effect and building suspense. We divide plays into small bits, and look for the action, we look for changes.

We know the key event in the scene we've been studying—it's when Constantine stops the play. But how can we make that moment really resonate? In part through everything we've been talking about: creating deep relationships, investing in all the given circumstances, creating stakes and exploding conflict. But you also can delay the event.

By this we mean that Constantine doesn't give up when his mother makes the first comment, he tries to quiet her, get her to invest, and push forward. Nina too must notice that people are talking or fidgeting during her performance, but she doesn't stop. In fact, the more that Arkadina interrupts, the more that the two lovers try to make the play work.

Then finally, Arkadina goes one step too far, making the proceedings into a farce and Constantine breaks. The dam bursts and he lets out all the frustration that built up over the course of the scene. If Arkadina quieted down, perhaps he would have let the play finish. But she says one more comment, he loses his temper, and the course of the play is altered forever. Nothing will be the same.

TRY THIS: CREATE A REHEARSAL CHECK LIST FOR A SCENE

- Look at a scene from a play and ask yourself some basic questions.
- Who is in the scene? What do they want from each other?
- What are ten key given circumstances that drive the scene?
- Where does it take place? When does it take place?

Now what questions are you left with? What will drive your curiosity as you work on the scene? What choices will you need to make when you work on the scene?

WORKING ON INTIMACY AND VIOLENCE

If your scene calls for violence of any kind, you need to slow this down and work through it beat by beat. You'll be creating some sort of staging that is safe for the actors but looks to the audience like someone is getting punched, or kicked, or dragged across the floor viciously. If possible, try to work with a certified fight director, someone who has explicit training in creating safe and exciting violence on stage. If you can't work with a fight director, is there anyone in your cast who has some stage combat training who can help with these scenes?

As you examine the violence that's suggested in the text, try to understand why the playwright called for a fight. Why do the characters stop speaking and erupt into punching each other or pulling out a weapon? Be clear with whoever is staging the violence and the actors why the scene exists in the play and how you plan to approach it.

When working on this moment, slow everything down, use caution, and be incredibly clear about each physical move. Your stage manager should write down complete and detailed notes on the fights so that they can monitor them for accuracy during rehearsals, run-throughs, and performances. Before each rehearsal or performance where you will encounter the violence—be sure to run a fight call where you explicitly run the combat slowly, and then up at show speed.

Intimacy is defined as any moment in the play where actors simulate some sort of romantic or sexual interaction. These moments should be just as clearly delineated as moments of violence or combat. Again, if you can find a trained intimacy coordinator to work with you on these moments, bring someone in to help guide you and the cast.

If you can't work with an intimacy coordinator, again, take your time, be over explicit about how you'll work on these scenes and check boundaries early and often with your actors. Step through these moments of intimacy with the same amount of care and precision as a fight. A stage manager should document every kiss or caress the same way they would detail every punch and kick.

Create a ritual around these moments of intimacy where the actors check in about their boundaries that day and agree to either review the moment step by step or at least talk through the moments clearly. By creating a culture of trust and communication around these moments, you'll build confidence in the company.

RUNNING THE PLAY

When I interviewed directors for my book *How to Rehearse a Play*, I was surprised how many different ways people employed run-throughs.

A run-through is simply when the cast starts at the beginning of the play and performs it until the end without stopping except for intermission breaks. I found directors employed some version of three methods: run early and often, run as late as possible, and the gradual build up strategy. As you listen to each of these examples, ask yourself, what style of director might I be? Which method excites me and makes sense?

Kimberly Senior, Broadway Director, runs her plays early and often. If she has a three-week rehearsal process before going into technical rehearsals, she will try to stage the play in the first week and a half so she can have ten full days of running the play every day.

She came to this idea when she was directing the Broadway production of *Disgraced* by Ayad Akhtar, a taut eighty-minute drama that explodes into chaos. She had an instinct the play was a sort of athletic event, and the actors needed to build up stamina. When the actors protested, perhaps nervous about monotony setting in, Senior suggested that they would have a different target for every run-through. One day they would target "finding the stakes" and next "be the best attorney for your character" followed by "love your partners."

Senior kept this model for her other plays, running often and assigning a target for each run-through. In this way, each run can reveal something new. She doesn't see a rehearsal process as one where the play gets better and better, quality moving upward like a line graph over time. Instead, she believes a play is like a painting, gathering layers over time, accumulating depth and meaning. (See Appendix 6 for a list of run-through targets.)

I don't run a show as many times as Senior does, but I tend to follow the advice of one of my grad school professors: Run the show once a week to see what you have.

DELAYING RUN-THROUGHS

Tony-award winning director, Ivo Van Hove, takes the opposite approach to Kimberly Senior. He runs the play for the first time as late as possible, working in intense detail moment by moment during the rehearsal process. Van Hove requires actors to be off book for the first day, puts people in costumes, has his sound designer bring in cues to play with, and rehearses on some semblance of the set. Then on the first day, he starts staging and working the scenes in minute detail.

Van Hove won't move forward on a scene until he deems it performance ready. He goes back over a scene many times trying many different ideas. He tests the staging, the rhythm, the use of props, the emotional attack, the use of language. He doesn't sketch in the outline and go back later; he works in fine detail. Working this slowly means sometimes he doesn't finish the entire play before it's time to move into the theatre and start technical rehearsals.

I don't follow Van Hove's advice, because I like to check in more often with the work to see what we've accomplished so far. I find I want to run after a first pass, then again after a second pass through the scenes.

BUILDING UP THE MUSCLES

Lisa Portes, Head of Directing at DePaul University, often employs a middle ground: she builds up her runs day by day.

The first day on their feet, the cast works from the beginning of the play until the end of the rehearsal. The next day they will start by reviewing what they did the day before, and then moving forward. The next day they review from the beginning, running from the top of the play, up to the point they stopped. Each day after follows the same pattern: run from the top to wherever they stopped. Then, a brief chat before moving forward.

Portes calls each day's partial run-through a "review." In the daily review, she encourages actors to look for new ideas, try new opportunities, and resist pressure to perform. It's not casual; it's a review with curiosity. Right before they go into tech, she tells her cast they are ready to run the play, to fully go for it as if it were a performance.

The one downside to this method is that each day, more and more of your rehearsal time will be taken up with the review, leaving less time for staging or work. The big upside is that your play should feel more and more secure in the actors' hands as they build up the muscles. Also, as actors learn more about the beginning of the play, they discover how to perform the end. They understand the journey.

ASSESSING YOUR WORK TO DATE

Why run the play from beginning to end? What purpose do run-throughs serve? How should you prepare for them and what should you do to follow up?

Obie Award winning director Robert O'Hara calls his run-through sessions landscape and triage. By landscape, he means that he looks out over the entire surface of the play. He's not caught up in every minute twist and turn, but instead sees it all at once.

At the end of the run, O'Hara asks his cast to write down three moments in the play they would like to examine more slowly. This is called triage—detailing what hurts. O'Hara also has his own triage list, moments that he thinks aren't working yet. The next day O'Hara works his triage list before they run the play again. At the end of the day's landscape review, O'Hara asks for another set of triage moments and the cycle repeats.

Most theatre companies schedule a designer run-through just before tech begins. If you're working in a professional setting, the artistic director will likely attend as well, and perhaps some other staff. In a university setting, academic advisors might come to the run to check the progress and give notes to the director.

When approaching this kind of run-through, many directors try to ratchet down the tension and help the actors feel at ease. I try to let the designers know that this is just one more rehearsal, we still have work to do, it's just a check of our progress. I also take the time to make sure we do a round of introductions, so everybody knows who's in the room.

How will you figure out what kind of run-through method you want to employ? Do you want to run as often as possible? Do you want to run once late in the process? Or do you want to build up the muscles? Perhaps you want to run once a week at the end of the week?

For your first time out, you may want to try this method: Run once a week for the first few weeks and run every day in the last week before tech. This combines some of the strengths of the different approaches, allowing you the chance to see the whole often in the process, and allowing your actors the ability to learn from repetition later in the process. But as you develop and grow as a director, know that this aspect of scheduling is in your control. What helps you and your cast learn the play best?

TECHNICAL REHEARSALS

Directing a play involves so much guessing, imagining, dreaming, and hoping. As you read the play you imagine who might be in it or how it might look. As you make design choices you make educated predictions about how the space will work, what clothes fit the characters, and how light and sound can tell the story.

In tech you stop speculating and start creating with all the tools at your disposal.

During tech you set all the design cues for the show, looking to tell the story and create beauty on stage. The designers create light and sound cues, and projection cues if you have those. The actors interact with all the props, wear the costumes, and work with the set. As a team you practice transitions from scene to scene and quick costumes changes. You learn everything you can without an audience and then present it to spectators.

Technical time builds excitement for the entire team but also causes stress and pressure. In just a few days an audience will arrive—will you finish everything in time? You have all the tools at your disposal, which increases the number of decisions to make quickly. Draw on the trust and collaboration that you have built up throughout the process. The more collaborative the design and rehearsal process, the more joyful the tech process.

I encourage you to fulfill three roles during tech: storyteller, time manager, and team leader.

TELLING THE STORY

Imagine working the transition from the end of Act 1 of *The Seagull* to the top of Act 2. We need to shift from one scene to the next and switch locations. At the end of Act 1 it's a muggy night and Dorn and Masha are standing near the makeshift stage. At the top of Act 2, a week or so has passed, we are on some sort of croquet lawn, it's sunny out, and Dorn, Masha, and Arkadina are sitting around relaxing. Imagine the transition runs and parts don't seem quite right. You could imagine saying something like this:

> I think you called the cue to start the transition at the end of Dorn's first line, you should take it at the end of the second line. That music seemed to get louder on a five count, could we try a ten count? Those blue lights from the side there, could we raise their level about fifty percent in the transition?

While you may get what you want, it's more likely you'll cause some confusion by controlling each of these aspects. Also, you're robbing artists of their creativity. I like to tell my students, "A director isn't in the cue calling or cue building business; they are in the story telling business." Instead imagine something like this:

> We want to really focus on Dorn and Masha for a moment, and experience her deep sadness, before we end this scene and start the transition. And then I think we want to gently step into this change rather than hurtle forward, we are moving forward a week and the slowness will help us, I think. And I'm hoping that the transition can feel a bit more magical? Or lyrical? Something to bounce off of Dorn's lines about a magical lake?

In this way you're opening a collaborative conversation with your team. They can ask you what you mean by lyrical or magical, or just show you something. They can take your description of what you're looking for and try to find their own ways to create it, perhaps surprising you with something you hadn't imagined.

TIME MANAGER

The play you are working on, as well as the amount of time you have will determine the type of tech you run and the pace you need to work. But you and the stage manager have some flexibility in terms of how fast or slow you move through cues. In interviews with directors, I found some liked to move very deliberately, not moving past a cue until it was perfect. These directors tended to get to a run-through later in the process, perhaps just before the first audiences or sometimes even at the first preview. Other directors like to race through the cues as quickly as possible so they can get to a run-through with enough time to go through the play a second or even third time, working problem sections as they go.

You might have a discussion with your stage manager and your design team to see what suits them best and how they'd like to work. Once you have a plan, the stage manager can set goals for the day of how many pages you'd like to get through, and then you can leave the minute-to-minute management of time to them, while you focus on story telling.

If you've decided that you want to rough in cues quickly— then you can help move things along. This involves the subtle art of figuring out when a cue is "close enough" and when it's not quite there. How will you know if a cue is roughed in enough to continue and how do you know if you need to work on it some more? Some of this will come from collaborative conversations with your team—seeing who thinks they need to work on something right now, and who thinks they can't make it better until they have more work time. Is it close enough to what we imagine so that we could effectively see it in a run-through? Then let's move on.

THE LEADER OF THE TEAM

By the technical rehearsals, hopefully you've rallied your entire creative team around a point of view. You started cultivating this vision during your first reads and analysis and changed and expanded as you worked with your designers. As you moved forward you made new discoveries and clarified the point of view of the production. At the first rehearsal you made some sort of speech, outlining your outlook on the play and its meaning. During rehearsal you and your team made more discoveries, uncovering new understanding.

You also raised some new questions that can't be answered without all the technical elements. Now the team comes together to keep heading in the same direction, keep clarifying the same point of view. The actors and designers should by now have a sense of the tone of the show, the pace, the mood, and they don't need you to make every single decision. Instead, everyone is trying to work together towards a common goal.

In this way you can lead the team and allow them to do their work, instead of doing everyone's job. While the sound designer and the lighting designer try to finesse their timing on a cue, you can pop down to the stage and give some notes to the actors or fine tune some blocking. When a section of the play doesn't quite work, you don't have to have the solution, you can just raise the question and perhaps a collaborator will have the best idea.

Thinking back to the beginning of the chapter, a great rehearsal process involves making as many specific choices as possible within the time allowed. A great leader knows to get input from collaborators, check their instincts, and then choose boldly.

Finally, you are ready for the final test: the audience.

SUMMARY

In this chapter we have introduced:

- Creating a flexible but practical rehearsal schedule
- Crafting an inspiring first day speech
- Building a world with the cast
  - Using table work to examine scenes
  - Steeping the team in dramaturgy and research
  - Moving and playing games to build ensemble
- Understanding the emotional power of different parts of the stage
- Creating a sketch of the staging

- Delving into scene work by asking questions about who, what, where, when, and why
- Leading technical rehearsals as a storyteller, time manager, and artistic leader.

FURTHER READING

Alexander Dean and Lawrence Carra's *Fundamentals of Play Direction* offers a very complete technical idea of stage direction as does Michael Bloom's *Thinking Like a Director*. Harold Clurman's *On Directing* and William Ball's *A Sense of Direction* are romantic and artistic views on leading a company towards a vision. Anne Bogart's *A Directors Prepares* and Peter Brook's *The Empty Space* offer inspirational philosophy about the underpinnings of great leadership.

Viola Spolin has been somewhat overlooked as a trailblazer in terms of the introduction of play into rehearsal and her books *Improvisation for the Theatre* and *Theater Games for Rehearsal: A Director's Handbook* are practical and clear.

Two books that offer quick ideas about different challenges a director faces are *Tips: Ideas for Directors* by Jon Jory and *Notes on Directing* by Frank Hauser and Russel Reich.

To rehearse scenes involves actor coaching, so a deep study of acting will help any director. Konstantin Stanislavski's *An Actor's Work* remains the seminal text for most acting training schools. Other sources include *Black Acting Methods* by Sharrell Luckett and Tia Shaffer, *The Actor and the Target* by Declan Donnellan, and Uta Hagen's *Respect for Acting*.

Finally, my book, *How to Rehearse a Play*, based on interviews with over forty directors, covers much of the material in this chapter in more depth, and ends with 21 exercises and check lists to improve your rehearsals.

HELPFUL WEBSITES

Sites for the unions of the various professionals involved in rehearsing a play:

Directors and Choreographers: www.sdcweb.org.
Actors and Stage Managers Union: www.actorsequity.org.
Violence and Fight Directors: www.safd.org.
Intimacy Coordinators and Directors: www.idcprofessionals.com and
    https://www.theatricalintimacyed.com.
United Scenic Artists for Designers: www.usa829.org.

6

OPENING

The finals days before opening a play inspire stress, panic, joy, and hopefully triumph. They may also feel bittersweet as you let go of your baby and let it out into the world.

Broadway and regional theatre director Kimberly Senior thinks about opening a play in terms of her physical location. When she works in the rehearsal room, she's close to the actors, maybe even up on her feet in the playing space. When technical rehearsals start, she moves to the middle of the theatre, as she tries to see the whole picture and work with her designers. When previews begin, she sits in the back of the house, as far away from the stage as possible. And finally, she exits the back of the theatre and leaves the show to run on its own without her. To direct a play well you need to slowly let go and hand the play over to your collaborators.

As you move towards opening a show, hopefully all the small decisions you've made along the way start to pay off. Ideas about costumes that you made months ago mesh with character choices and staging. Hunches about how transitions will work with lights, sound, and people play out in real time.

At this point, as the audience approach, you probably don't have time to make huge changes. This is a moment for refining and editing. Peter Brook, in his seminal book, *The Empty Space*, wrote that directors work in two modes. In the beginning directors encourage creativity of all kinds, generating as many ideas as possible. As

DOI: 10.4324/9781003016922-6

rehearsals heads toward opening night, the director cuts out anything extraneous, and homes in on choices that tell the story clearly and with heart.

In this chapter, we'll focus on the final days of the process, finishing up technical rehearsals, previews, opening, and closing the show. We will cover:

- Receiving suggestions from others
- The art of giving notes
- Watching the show with an audience
- Leaving the building
- Filtering criticism

The length of this final process depends heavily on the type of theatre and the schedule. A Broadway show could have anywhere between two to five weeks of previews. In this process the creative team might change anything: script, blocking, lights and sound cues, even set and costume pieces. The entire company will likely rehearse changes during the day, and then perform at night. In a regional theatre, this process might be cut down to just a few days and in an academic institution you might not have any meaningful time for changes at all. You might move from tech, to opening, to a one week run, to closing.

Even with a shortened process, you can practice the art of opening a show gracefully.

THE ART OF RECEIVING SUGGESTIONS FROM OTHERS

When I am hired for a professional show, one of the first questions I ask is: "Who will give me notes and when?" In some cases, the theatre company has a clear system in place, and I know I'll get observations from the artistic director at the first run-through, at the first tech run-through, and all throughout previews.

An artistic director, or anyone giving notes, stands in for the audience. When you work on a play, you and the cast and creative team try out ideas and reject them. You make choices about character, blocking, and design. Many of these come in the moment and you all remember the progress that has been made. An audience doesn't know anything about your breakthroughs—they only see the show once. A good artistic collaborator serves as an impartial eye, giving their impressions of how an audience might view the show.

Before rehearsals being, I talk with the artistic director about the play, sharing my vision and making sure I understand how it works in their season. Given this sense of common ground, when I receive suggestions for improvement late in the process, they feel like a continuation of this artistic discussion rather than a set of demands from my boss.

If there is no one assigned to give notes and the artistic director isn't available, I try to arrange for someone else to come and watch at key points. I trust my work as a director, but I always have blind spots, and fresh eyes can help me find them.

A colleague of mine came to see a show I directed right before previews and noted that I was only using about one-third of the stage. I grouped most of my scenes down center and wasn't using the large and detailed set. I both bored the audience and gave each scene the same dramatic weight. Overwhelmed at first, I rallied to figure out which scenes needed to move in a single day of re-staging. Their outside eye allowed me to see the whole.

In an academic setting, you hopefully receive observations and suggestions from an advisor or a professor who knows your actors, your process, and the show. They can give ideas on how to improve the play and act as a sounding board. There may be problems you don't know how to fix, and they might have suggestions for what to bring back into rehearsal.

I encourage you to empower your collaborators to give you notes. If you have a dramaturg or an assistant director, give them specific tasks to look out for. Notes don't need to be scary or confrontational if you think of them as collaborative suggestions for making the play better.

FINDING THE SIGNAL THROUGH THE NOISE

When someone gives me notes, I like to physically sit down with them. This way if I don't understand something, we can talk it out. I can also filter out notes that aren't that helpful. In general, I'm wary of people offering solutions. I'm much more interested in hearing where they are confused or bored, and then working with my creative team for solutions.

This chapter focuses on opening a play, but you're likely to get notes at three points in your process:

- First full run-through
- First technical run-through
- Previews

If you can, ask for different kinds of notes at each point of this journey. Just before a run-through, let your viewers know where you are in the process, and what they can look out for. People coming to a first run shouldn't be bothering you with details. And at the final preview hopefully someone isn't telling you to change the entire arc of a character. What are the most helpful notes that you should ask for at different points in the journey?

After your first run-through ask for these observations:

- Character development—do you know who these people are?
- Relationships—are the actors finding clarity in their channel work?
- The general shape of the show physically—are you using one part of the stage too much? Is there flow?
- The general tone of the show—if it's a comedy, is it funny?
- Story clarity—do you understand how events process in the plot?
- Any places they were confused or bored?

After a first run-through you have time for big changes. A scene that was conceived of as busy perhaps can calm down. If you are missing a comic tone in a section, you can work on that in the coming weeks. If a character is vague and fuzzy, with unclear motivations, you can sharpen and specify.

After a technical run-through, ask for practical notes:

- Sightlines—are there any parts of your play that are obscured from certain parts of the house?
- Transitions—are they clean and elegant or a mess?
- Sound levels—can the actors be heard over underscoring. Is the music impacting the audience when it should?

- Lighting clarity—can the actors be seen? And do we know the time of day, place, and season?
- Costumes—do they tell a coherent story? Are the actors wearing them well?

Helpful notes consider how much tech time you have left. If your advisor or artistic director shows up on the final day and give you pages of notes—you won't be able to do anything with them. Hopefully they come to you with enough time that you and your team can prioritize the major notes and accomplish them before audiences arrive. If they don't, take a deep breath, look through the notes, and decide for yourself what you can accomplish. Store the rest of the notes away, read them after the play closes, and look for lessons for your next directing project.

And finally, during previews (if you are lucky enough to have them), ask for notes about details, moments, and audience impact:

- Pacing—this is the key moment to really manage the pace of the show, while in most cases faster is likely better, some scenes want to breathe.
- Clarity—can the actors be heard? Can the key gestures and movement be seen?
- Moment—are the key events, the ones you identified in your moment chain, landing on the audience?
- Story—What narrative is being told?
- Connection—Do we care? Are we emotionally invested?

Your ability to make changes once previews begin depends entirely on your situation. If you have work time, prioritize the most important changes first and leave details for later. If you only have time for note sessions, don't overwhelm your actors, but pick and choose to help them to the finish line. If you don't really have any time at all, store these notes away to look at after the play closes, and see them as lessons for future productions.

FILTERING NOTES THROUGH YOUR POINT OF VIEW

As the director of the show, it's important that all notes to actors or designers go through you. You are the final arbiter of which comments are important, and which can be put aside. You also want to guard against anyone giving notes to actors or designers directly. At the simplest level, you and your collaborators have developed a language over months and weeks, and while a note from someone else may be well meaning, they might be completely misunderstood.

I find that listening to notes just as you're opening the show can cause the most stress. Different people may have different solutions for problems, and time is running out.

Go back to your original impulses for doing the project and your analysis. What is the play about for you? Why did you choose it? How do you want it to impact the audience? What is the key question you're examining? Why do we care about these characters and what they are suffering? Where is there beauty and joy?

Now, which of these notes will help you achieve your vision?

TRY THIS: COMPOSING NOTES FOR A PRODUCTION

- Go see any production, and imagine the director asked you for notes.
- After the show, write down a series of observations.
- What questions did you have about the story?
- What concerns did you have about the staging or the characters?
- How could you give these notes in a constructive way?

What did you learn about watching the play with the note taking lens? Can you start to understand what would be helpful advice to a director?

THE ART OF GIVING NOTES

As you approach opening night, your main job will be watching the entire show, deciding what can and can't be changed, and effectively communicating with the actors and designers.

Many directors I spoke to described giving notes to actors as an art form they continued to develop over the course of their career.

Give a note too early, and you may frustrate an actor who is still developing their character. Give a note too late, and the actor may not have time to adjust. Give a bunch of notes around a scene and you may end up confusing everyone. Think about working on your craft of giving notes in three areas.

- Timing
- Clarity
- Tone

Again, you give feedback throughout the process, but I focus on note giving in this section because as you head to opening—the well-crafted note is your best friend.

TIMING THE NOTES

Learning how to time a note comes from uncovering the slightly different process of each of your actors. Giving notes about pace early in the process can stymie actors, but they need encouragement to speed up as opening approaches. Often actors build their performances from the inside out—so you'll want to help them discover relationships, action, conflict, and given circumstances first. Later you can move on to pace and diction, and finally to crafting small moments.

If I was directing a production of *The Seagull*, I could imagine my notes developing along these lines. After a first run-through I might give these kinds of notes:

- Paulina and Dorn—Remember your first encounter is a stolen moment—you might get discovered—how does that affect the scene?
- Arkadina—Continue to fight for people to be on your side after you stop the play.
- Nina/Constantine—Great work trying to relate to each other as old friends, keep on this track.
- Trigorin—When you are called back to the house, the clock starts ticking on your exit—raise the stakes.
- Paulina—Remember, this may be the last time you see your friend Arkadina for over a year, and you'll be stuck out here alone.

After a run-through closer to tech, notes may be more like this:

- Sorin/Constantine—You can tighten up those cues in the first scene and look for that cut off energy.
- Shamrayev—Remember to let that pause after your line ring out—don't move until Dorn finally speaks to break the tension.
- Masha—See if you can find some time on your own to practice pouring those drinks—we need to tighten that sequence up.

And finally, after a preview my notes are a combination of reminders and technical advice. Hundreds of tiny adjustments help a production affect an audience.

Some common notes I look out for:

- **Don't play the end of the scene at the beginning:** As actors work on the play, they will of course know the outcome of scenes, or acts. But as they play the scene, they need to rediscover the surprise each time.
- **Rediscover the moment:** Finding a moment in rehearsal is a great feeling, and actors love it. Sometimes they will try to recreate the feeling rather than play the action and be alive to their partner.
- **Take out the air:** Great playwrights are very specific about where they want pauses. If it's not written in, don't mess with the rhythm.
- **Energy to the end of the line:** Sometimes actors, especially students, will have great energy at the top of the line, but peter out in the middle. All the important stuff is usually at the end of the sentence, so they need to drive to the period.
- **Couldn't hear or couldn't understand:** It's not always about being louder—often just crisping up consonants can aid the clarity. Try Viola Spolin's favorite note: *Share with the audience.*

CLARITY OF NOTES

Mark Twain was quoted as saying: If you want me to speak for two hours, I'm ready now. If you want me to speak for five minutes, I'll need two weeks to prepare. It's easy to blather on for a while about something, groping towards your point, but to say something clear and impactful takes careful editing time.

Clarity emerges when you know what you want to say and remove clutter that obscures your message. When you are working on a scene with an actor in the rehearsal room, you might be able to ramble a bit and talk around the point. You might get in a conversation with the actor and together discover the problem and a possible solution.

When you give notes, cut to the point. With the technical notes we discussed above, these can be discerned easily and given simply. You want the actor to speak up, pick up their cue, make their entrance on time, leave more gracefully. If a scene lacks tension, perhaps it can be solved by reminding actors of a key given circumstance. If actors have forgotten or let slip some motivation or action you all worked on—hopefully a quick nudge will prompt them back on course.

TONE OF NOTES

Frank Hauser and Russell Reich, in their book *Notes on Directing*, offer many lovely suggestions on how to speak to actors. They encourage leading from a place of collaboration and positivity. They even suggest changing the word "but" to "and." A note that might first come out as, "We love that hat, but we can't see your face if you tip your head down" becomes, "We love that hat, and we'll see your face better if you tip your head up." The goal here is to get actors to do something, not get in their head about not doing something.

Also, especially as you get closer to opening, give more and more positive notes. Build confidence in the material and their performances. You should beware undoing weeks of work with a general note about a scene. Instead, praise specific moments, and help them sharpen little things that need work. If we think back to the very beginning of the whole book—your job is to lead everyone to the final product—not to act the show for them.

HOW TO DISTRIBUTE NOTES TO ACTORS

After your early run-throughs, I encourage you to circle up and have a check in. Ask the actors to go around and briefly say how it went.

You'll gather the general mood and learn where each person is in their process. Probably you'll hear many of the notes you were thinking of giving. After this check in—give your notes clearly but make sure you allow folks the time to question or get in a conversation. These notes sessions should build clarity as a team of where you are heading.

Later in the process, you may run out of time to give notes in person. In this case, you may want to type up notes and email them out to actors. Be forewarned; this will take you a fair amount of time. You'll need to translate your scribblings during a run-through into coherent and actionable language. I've seen some directors who have great handwriting use a notecard system, handing out notes at the end of a run. If I have an assistant director, I whisper notes in their ear as they type away on a computer.

If possible, check in with each actor and ask them how they would like to receive notes. Are they okay getting a mass email? Would they rather get a personal message? Would they like to meet you in person for five minutes to clarify emailed notes? Would they rather get a phone call where you give your notes in person? You'll save time in the long run if you give notes the way the actors want them, because they'll be received more clearly.

And finally—feedback needs to come well before any performance. Actors need time—at least a few hours if not a full day, to process notes, think about them, and then hopefully forget them before they perform.

GIVING NOTES TO DESIGNERS

Your work with designers will likely move from the general to the specific. During tech time hopefully you sorted out roughly what scenes should look like, how transitions should sound and move, and what people are wearing. During the final days when you are watching run-throughs, notes should be about small moments and technical matters.

Keep in mind the same skills you developed with your actors— shooting for notes that are clear, uplifting in tone, specific, and well timed. During your final days your notes to the lighting designer hopefully aren't, this whole scene is dark, but instead that you can't see an actor's face on a certain line. With a sound designer, you'll be refining levels and timing. With a stage manager, you'll be checking to see if they missed a cue or if it needs to be moved earlier. Again, just like with actors, ask each designer how they want to get their notes.

WATCHING THE SHOW WITH AN AUDIENCE

When Obie Award winning director Anne Kauffman finishes up technical rehearsals, she jokes with her cast that when previews start, that's when rehearsal will really begin. It's a joke because of course they've been rehearsing for weeks, figuring out staging, character work, and technical details. But the grain of truth lies in Kauffman's belief that she really doesn't understand a play until she sees it with an audience.

Kauffman was one of many directors who told me that during the preview process, they would learn about the play from the audience, and sometimes make drastic changes. Perhaps they misunderstood that the opening needed to have a lighter tone to set people up for the rest of the evening. Something funny in rehearsal fell flat in performance.

The job of the director during previews is to watch the play with new eyes, prioritize what needs improvement, and use whatever time they have left to make final adjustments. In your case you may have absolutely no work time during previews. Maybe you have a preview or two and then a chance to give notes. In this case, really think hard about what can be changed with quick email and what needs work time. It's probably smart to be conservative in these final note sessions, trust your actors and the process, and give mostly positive feedback.

What if you have absolutely no preview time at all? What if you go straight from tech to performances? In this case I encourage you to take notes you will never give. It may frustrate you, but you are practicing your craft. Anything you learn about watching a show with audiences on this production will pay off on your next one.

How do you watch a show with an audience?

WATCHING THE SHOW WITH NEW EYES

As you watch the show listen for a few tell-tale signs: laughter, gasps, stillness, and rustling. As you watch the show over several nights you see where the audience always laughs, and where there are different reactions. Gasps for exciting moments are the same—clear indicators the show is working.

If you aren't getting laughs where you expected, go back to the situation—are the actors looking for a laugh, or playing the truth of the moment? The actors need to invest in the given circumstance, work towards their objectives, and truly be surprised or frustrated by the results. Comedy comes from discovery—and if you don't ever get the laugh—at least you are telling the story well.

Now observe when the audience seems to hold their breath together or really focus in on a moment. This is another indication that the play is working. But when you hear lots of coughing or rustling—the audience is bored, confused, or both. Why? Even if you won't have time to fix these sections, practice figuring out what might be wrong:

- Are the actors speaking clearly, in a way that the audience can understand?
- Does the audience understand the basic situation (a breakup, a performance, a lesson)?
- Does the audience know what's at stake? Do they care?
- Is the scene too busy? Are actors moving too much?
- Is the focus correct? Do audiences know where to look?
- Are the actors playing in the moment or are they ahead of the scene?

When you rehearse a play, everyone watches the show over and over. You experience many versions of the same moment. An audience only has one shot to see the play and they must understand the situation, learn who the characters are, start to care about the people, and invest in the problems of the play. All without any prior knowledge. Trust the reactions of a preview audience to tell you where you need to sharpen your story telling.

PRIORITIZING WORK DURING PREVIEWS

Even if you don't have work time, after a night of watching your play ask yourself: what would I do if I had another week of rehearsal?

Three days? One day? Two hours? During the show you'll take many notes, some mental, some physical. You can't give them all—if you did, the actors would only think about your notes and never be in the moment.

When I do have work time during a preview process, I sometime like to pull out my moment chain for the last time. As you'll remember from Chapter 2 this is a list of the two dozen or so most important moments in the play. I look through the moment chain and ask myself—which of these events land with the audience? Which float by without making an impact? Which moments confuse the actors?

After every preview, the actors go home, and the design gathers to check in. The director gives notes to the team and draws up a work list. Each designer shares notes that impact the group. At this point the stage manager can help prioritize the next day as they have a sense of how fast each person on the team works.

LEAVING THE BUILDING

Even if you only have a run of a week or a few days, I encourage you to not attend at least one or two of the performances. The actors and stage managers need a sense that they own the show and can do it without supervision. You can't change what's happening on stage anyway, so best to give it some freedom.

Before you go, make sure that you deputize your stage manager to maintain the show for the length of the run. At the bare minimum, the stage manager needs to preserve the blocking, script, and timing. If an actor starts to seriously stray from the staging that was set, they need to get them back on track. If actors start to add pauses or time to the show, then the stage manager needs to have a conversation and bring the performance on pace.

You might want to give some final remarks on opening night, or the last rehearsal. This kind of speech signals to the company that you've completed your job, you trust them and love their work, and you can't wait to experience the show as an audience member. You finished your job.

FILTERING CRITICISM

Once people see your play, they form opinions. Some of those judgments will reach your ears and eyes. These opinions may come in the form of reviews in a campus newspaper or a local media source or a theatre blog. More likely you'll receive either formal or informal feedback from fellow students, teachers, advisors, and even friends and relatives. Don't let these critiques affect the run of the show.

I would encourage telling the cast that critiques, reviews, and opinions should be kept out of the dressing room. If people praise a certain moment in the play, actors can start to play to the praise rather than live in the moment. Worse still, if people hear negative opinions about their acting, they may take it upon themselves to fix their performance. Encourage your cast to trust the work and let each audience see the show you all made.

If you read a review or hear a critique and go back to your show, you may start to view the production entirely through that lens and despair. If possible, try to keep critiques at bay until after the close of the production. If you can't help hearing or reading something about the show, try to view these opinions as one of many.

After the production closes, you may want to have one or more postmortems to evaluate your own work.

LISTENING TO A POSTMORTEM

Postmortem comes from the Latin and literally means, after death. In the theatre, the postmortem is a chance to evaluate the entire production with the benefit of hindsight. If you are in an academic setting, there may be a formal process set up. If not, try to organize one yourself and find someone you trust to lead the discussion. I encourage setting up some sort of guidelines so you get the feedback you need.

Liz Lerman, world-renowned choreographer and speaker developed the Critical Response Process to help artists receive useful feedback in the early stages of creating new pieces. The Process creates dialogue that is helpful to the creators, getting people to engage with the show that was created, rather than the one they would direct themselves. The feedback moves in steps:

- **What do you remember?**
  - People are encouraged to speak about images and moments that come back to them immediately. At first trying to give no judgement at all—just the lines, images, and moments that made an impression.
- **What was meaningful?**
  - People are encouraged to share what they loved about the piece. What moved them? What affected them emotionally or intellectually?
- **Questions from the artist.**
  - At this point the director would ask specific questions about the piece they wanted to hear about. Things they were obsessing over in the process. For example, you could ask, "Did you feel sympathy for Arkadina at any point in the play? When? Why?"
- **Neutral Questions from the viewers.**
  - Audience members are encouraged to ask questions about the piece they truly are curious about. They should be guided to avoid opinions that are disguised as questions. For example, "Why didn't Nina act more out of control in the last act?" is less helpful than "What was Nina's mental state like in the last act for you?"
- **Opinions.**
  - In the Critical Response Process as outlined by Lerman, this section is guarded by the artist. An audience member might say, "I have an opinion about your use of the Seagull prop, do you want to hear it." And the artist can say either no or yes depending on whether they are interested.

Whether you use this kind of response format or some other design for your postmortem, the most important task for the person leading the discussion is to guide people to engage with the piece that was made. Too often these discussions can devolve into people offering opinions about how to re-direct the play for you after the fact, which is less helpful.

REFLECTING ON REFLECTIONS

After the production is over, and you've gathered reflections from several people, and some time has passed, take a moment to look over all the critiques. What lessons can be learned for your next production?

Be sure to celebrate your successes. What did you set out to achieve that you accomplished? What surprises did you encounter along the way? What did you create that was a beautiful revelation?

As you sift through the questions and critiques, see if there is some sort of pattern. Do most people agree that one section lagged in pace or didn't capture their interest? Think about that section. Do you agree? Or what might you do differently next time? If on the other hand only one person has an opinion about a section, regardless of how strongly they felt or how much status they hold—you can hold those comments at arm's length and examine them.

You know best where you outdid your own expectations and where you came up short. Try to analyze why you succeeded. What are your natural talents or developed skills in directing? Don't take these for granted and nurture their development. Where did you fall short? Why? What knowledge might you lack, or skills do you need to develop?

As we discussed at the beginning of the book, great directors spend their whole life learning about theatre. They always seek ways to improve their process and deepen their understanding. As you move through life as an artist continue to ask the question: Why am I a director?

SUMMARY

In this chapter we discussed opening a play, while looking back at some other aspects of the process. We introduced:

*   Receiving suggestions during the process
*   Giving notes to actors and designers

- Watching the show with audiences
- Leaving the production in the hands of the actors and stage managers
- Processing critical feedback

FURTHER READING

Theatrical Memoirs are a great way to read about opening nights, runs of plays, and critical feedback. *Theatre in the Round* by Margo Jones charts her career in Texas as she attempts to start one of the first regional theatres in the United States. *My Life in Art* by Konstantin Stanislavski is a wide-ranging book, starting with his childhood and ending with old age, and it's an astonishing portrait of an artist who was never satisfied and always looking to improve his craft. *The Impact of Race: Theatre and Culture* by Woodie King, Jr. details his decades long attempt to create lasting Black and African American theatre. Andre Gregory's *This is Not my Memoir*, is a fascinating look at one person's very long journey.

HELPFUL WEBSITES

Sometimes reading a bunch of reviews around a show can help you understand how a production has been received from different perspectives. After you see a show, if there are many reviews, read them all and see what you agree with. You might even read reviews of a show that you can't see, just to practice sifting through critiques. Some review aggregators:

New York Reviews: www.didhelikeit.com.
Chicago Reviews: www.theatreinchicago.com.
London: www.thestage.co.uk.com.

DEVISING

How do you devise a play?

To devise a show an ensemble starts a rehearsal process without a script and creates material together. Actors write scenes, designers improvise moments, and directors guide the collaboration. This process takes weeks, months, or even years.

Ensembles begin with different launch pads depending on their interests. Some companies start with nothing but physical improvisations and then see if a theme arises organically. Others begin with a myth and then fashion their own version. Others might look to a historical figure for inspiration, bringing in research on their life and times. Sometimes companies start with a piece of fiction or even a classic play, but then create dialogue that is all their own.

In this chapter I introduce you to a few theatre companies that start rehearsals without a set script. If one group intrigues you, check out their website and investigate their work. Some companies filmed documentaries about their process, and others have written books, or offer workshops.

A devising process often follows three phases, which is how we'll divide the chapter:

- The spark
- Generating material
- Workshopping the show

DOI: 10.4324/9781003016922-7

Why might you want to devise a piece of theatre rather than working from a script? Perhaps you want to tell a specific story that hasn't been written yet. Are you interested in creating a piece that relies more on movement or designed moments rather than text? On a practical level, it could be you don't want to do a classic play in the public domain, but you don't want to pay for rights for an existing script. A devised piece of theatre doesn't need to be a full length two act evening of theatre. It could be simply five to twenty minutes of a performance. Or even just a three-minute piece for class.

To start a devised piece of theatre you need a launching pad, a hunch, a germ of an idea. You need a spark to start the process.

THE SPARK

The Tectonic Theater Project creates theatre through their devising process called Moment Work, which relies on a spark to start the process. In October of 1998, Matthew Shepard, a gay college student, was tortured, beaten, and left to die in Laramie Wyoming. The news reverberated around the country, raising alarms about anti-gay violence. The artistic director of Tectonic, Moisés Kaufman, wondered how theatre might respond. Could their company of artists add to the national dialogue? A group of ensemble members flew to Laramie with recording equipment and set out to interview members of the town. He and Barbara Pitt McAdams detail their process in *Moment Work: Tectonic Theater's Process for Devising Theater.*

These actors, directors, and writers didn't have any formal journalistic expertise but were driven by their desire to understand what happened. They fanned out around the small city, working to gain the trust of local citizens, gathering their thoughts about the town, Shepard, and the violence.

When two men were charged for the murder, with suspicions they had killed Shepard because he was gay, the Tectonic ensemble members returned to Laramie for the trial. Once again, they interviewed subjects, observed the town, attended the trial, and immersed themselves in the events. They generated hours of taped interviews and hundreds of pages of transcripts.

When they started the process, the ensemble didn't know what form the piece would take, or how they would use the transcripts, or even what narrative they were drawn to. They just had a hunch that there was a story to tell on stage.

THE SPARK OF PERSONAL HISTORY

In their book, *Ensemble-Made Chicago: A Guide to Devised Theatre*, Coya Paz Brownrigg and Chloe Johnston explore fifteen theatre companies that create work in Chicago. For each company they describe a moment from a production, give a brief history, and then describe some of their devising exercises. One company exemplifies using personal histories as the spark for creating a show: About Face Youth Ensemble.

About Face Theatre Company was founded in 1995 in Chicago to uplift gay and lesbian stories and artists. In 1998, the murder of Matthew Shepherd rocked the About Face company members just as it had spurred the folks at Tectonic Theater Project. They decided to formalize their education department and create the About Face Youth Ensemble.

In 1999 the Youth Ensemble devised their first show, loosely based on company members' stories of coming out and falling in love. In the following years, youth company members interviewed older members of the LGBTQ community forging rare cross-generational stories. Every season the Youth Ensemble drives the quest to find a theme or topic to investigate, explore, and use for creative inspiration. They devised pieces about gay homelessness, gender issues in the undocumented community, and online places of refuge.

Over the decades, the ensemble conceived novel ways to inspire each other to create content. In a warmup exercise called Vending Machine, participants state their name, their gender pronouns, and what they would vend if they were a machine. "My name is Damon, he/him, and right now I would vend hugs for my kids!" For another exercise, ensemble members pair off and tell each other personal stories. They gather into groups of four, share the anecdotes and pick one to stage, making sure to protect the identity of the original story teller.

If you think you'd like to devise a work based on personal histories, consider looking through *Ensemble-Made Chicago*, *Moment Work*, *The Viewpoints Book*, or any other number of books that outline devised work processes. You could create your own exercises to encourage your ensemble members to share personal stories and then transform them into theatrical material. Some key ideas to consider:

- People should only share what they are comfortable talking about.
- Keep the process moving, writing sessions should probably be five to ten minutes to keep people in their bodies and not their heads.
- Consider transforming any story you create into something physical.
- Encourage people to not perform as themselves, but instead take on other people's stories.
- Develop a sense of "Yes, And" meaning if a person makes a proposal for a scene, the ensemble will join them and try to keep it going.
- Be aware that people may be emotional or sensitive seeing moments from their lives reflected back to them.

Finally, you probably don't want to jump into this work right away, but instead spend time building trust. Look through games and exercises from Augusto Boal or Viola Spolin and see what inspires you. Games can include anything from playing catch with an imaginary ball, mirroring each other's movements, speaking to each other in gibberish, or creating imaginary machines with just the actors' bodies.

Don't move on to creating content or soliciting stories until the group feels confident with each other physically, emotionally, and instinctually. As you start your work looking for stories, consider starting each rehearsal with warmup and ensemble building games.

A SPARK CAN COME FROM ANYWHERE

You don't need to pull from your own personal history or from a moment from the past to find a spark. Ensembles that devise often speak about not knowing exactly where the next piece will come from but trusting their instincts. Many companies talk about chance encounters, unfiltered conversations, and unfounded hunches guiding their process.

What is nagging you at this point? What do you feel is begging for a theatrical exploration? Or what types of movement or music or dancing do you want to explore? If you're devising a piece, talk to a potential ensemble of actors and designers. If they are going to play with you for weeks or longer, you'll want to choose something that animates everyone.

Your next step involves taking your spark of an idea and making it physical. You'll create theatrical moments as a group and start writing your piece in space and time.

TRY THIS: FIND A SPARK FOR DEVISING

- Is there a person or event from the past that you are obsessed with?
- Are you spurred by a recent political moment?
- Ask yourself a series of questions about that event or person.
- As you keep asking questions, is there a deeper question at the center?

Can you generate many questions, or do you run out of steam? Do you quickly come to some sort of conclusion or is your curiosity deepened? Can you imagine bringing this idea to a group of friends or classmates?

GENERATING MATERIAL

How do you create material for a play if you don't have a script?

Every theatre company devises in their own way. Some refined a method for creating shows over years and decades, and now follow a formula of sorts from first idea to opening night. Other companies have no specific method for creating material, and count on each other as a group. They know that if they put themselves in a room with some time to play, something will come out on the other side.

Most theatre companies that devise shows know you need to generate a lot of material during workshops and rehearsals, with the understanding that the vast majority will get cut. What are companies creating? Anything that might be a part of a theatrical performance:

- Dialogue and monologues
- Songs
- Dances
- Puppet Shows
- Movement pieces
- Moments that involve music, lights, costumes, props, or projections

Generating material in a devising process relies on improvisations, which means that performers have some rules and a degree of freedom. Actors find creativity with boundaries. Let's look at devising processes from a few theatre companies for example of how to structure spontaneity.

MOMENT WORK

In their book, *Moment Work*, Moisés Kaufman and others from the Tectonic Theater Project outline the devising method they refined over many years. They start with the belief that "moments" are what make theatre memorable and exciting—not plot, dialogue, or character.

Think about the theatrical experiences you loved the most. What comes back to you right now? What do you remember? Kaufman would suggest that likely you don't remember a bit of dialogue in a show or a plot twist, but a theatrical moment. Some short burst of time where you felt your senses engage, your breath quicken, and your sense of presence heighten.

I remember a key moment from a show I saw in high school. Robert Falls directed Shakespeare's *Hamlet* for a theatre company called Wisdom Bridge. In the middle of the play, Hamlet gives a crucial speech about whether he should stay alive or possibly take his own life. In the production, Falls had Hamlet spray paint the words "To be" on the wall, and then turn to the audience and say, "or not to be" and then went on to do the rest of the speech. I'll never forget the sound of the spray paint, the shock of this young punk Hamlet defacing the actual theatre wall, and the suspense we all felt as he was painting.

Kaufman suggests instead of reading a play, thinking how to interpret it, and discovering theatrical events, why not start with the moments? Why not create the thing that will resonate with an audience, and then write the dialogue? Why not start with spray painting the wall rather than the speech? Tectonic suggests that you write with the language of theatre, rather than with words. What "speaks" on stage?

- Props
- Lights
- Sound
- Costumes
- Movement
- Silence
- Color
- Gesture
- Puppets
- Voice

You could on your own continue this list of the countless things that impact an audience. These things will include character, story, emotion, and dialogue, but Kaufman suggests starting with less common elements first.

If you challenged a group of actors to create moments that featured light as a theatrical element, you could imagine them taking fifteen minutes to play, then coming back and presenting to the group one by one. You could envision the following moments happening:

- Someone lit only by their phone, scrolling through their news feed
- A person slowly raising the blinds in the room
- A dark space, a closet door cracks open briefly, opens fully, silhouetting someone, the light goes out
- Two people drifting towards and away from a window simultaneously

Eventually as people start to play with theatrical elements, they will combine to create moments out of light and music, or text and gesture. You could ask performers to string a few moments together or combine two moments into a third creation. As the ensemble starts to gravitate around a few key moments, now someone can start writing dialogue and scenes to contextualize what they've created.

TRY THIS: REMEMBERING THEATRICAL MOMENTS

- Think about the favorite shows you've seen in your lifetime.
- What moments stick out to you?
- Is there a specific moment that is especially clear? Can you describe it fully?
- Why does this moment stick with you?

What elements of theatre were in play in this moment? Can you break apart the moment and discover why it worked?

COMPOSITION WORK

Anne Bogart extols the virtues of "exquisite pressure"; give artists too many tasks and not enough time to create a piece of theatre. Pressure encourages collaborators to avoid talking too much, get out of their heads, and start just creating on their feet. Exquisite pressure forms the backbone of Composition Work.

As outlined in *The Viewpoints Book*, Composition work serves as a companion to Viewpoints training, which helps actors develop instinctual abilities to improvise physically. Composition exercises consist of a group of collaborators creating short theatrical pieces by working together to solve a set of tasks. It's a way for an ensemble to write as a group in time and space, rather than on a piece of paper. The process demands quick intuitive work and encourages leaderless creation.

Here is an imagined Composition Assignment:

- Your piece should have four parts: 1. The Beginning of the Journey; 2. Getting Lost; 3. Magical Help; 4. Finding Home
- The piece should be made in a found space—meaning some part of the building not typically designed for theatre

- The following ingredients must be part of the composition in any order:
  - A surprise entrance
  - Discovery of an object
  - A space revealed in a different light
  - Three uses of light
  - Sound used in at least four different ways
  - A staged accident
  - A gesture repeated ten times
  - A reference to a TikTok video
  - Underscoring
  - Stillness
  - Frantic motion
  - Unison action for at least 20 seconds
  - Five lines of text
- You need to create something that you can repeat easily
- You have thirty minutes

If Moment work asks performers to isolate theatrical vocabulary, Composition work overloads performers with many types of theatrical language at once. Composition work inundates collaborators intentionally, pushing them to work from a place of impulse rather than intellect.

Bogart and the SITI Company have used Composition work to create devised work by exploring themes and ideas on their feet. Rather than starting with a completely written script, they start with a hunch and then gather as much material as possible. Once they have text, images, and ideas: they start to create compositions.

GROUP AUTHORSHIP

How can a group without a set playwright create scenes for actors?

The PigPen Theatre Company writes plays through a communal process, relying on what they call a Quaker Consensus; all seven members must agree on something before it goes into a production. Their shows always contain American Roots infused songs, various forms of puppetry, and epic storytelling.

When they were creating *The Hunter and the Bear* in 2016, they started with a notion for a frontier ghost story about a father who ventures into the darkest parts of the woods when his son goes missing after a bear attack. They launched the process with a two-week session working with puppets, writing songs, and playing—but not writing any dialogue. PigPen believes storytelling can come from many places, not just spoken language, so they wanted to start with the more theatrical elements.

Their next session focused on writing a first draft of the play, incorporating the songs, puppetry, and other theatrical ideas they generated. They crafted an outline and created storyboards. All seven of them worked together, discussing, drawing, revising, arguing, and eventually agreeing on the shape of the story.

Next, they started writing scenes, using their outline. Sometimes they would create a Google document and all seven would take out their laptops and write the scene together. Other times they split up into three mini writing groups, each team comparing their creations after a set time. Sometimes one group's scene was clearly the best version. Other times they would take the beginning of the scene from group A, the middle from group B, and the ending from group C.

After two weeks together the group had a first draft of the script, including original songs, movement sequences, and places for shadow and large-scale puppetry. They were ready to go into rehearsal.

DISCOVERING YOUR OWN WAY TO GENERATE MATERIAL

Moment work, Composition work, and group authorship are only a few examples of the countless ways to generate theatrical material. Remember that the point of devising is to create as many theatrical moments as possible, without much judgment. If you think of a devised play as a script that will have fifty pages, assume you need to create 200–500 pages of material at first. Also remember that "pages" of a devised piece might include a song, or a dance, or a fight, or a moment of puppetry.

Why improvise material? Why work from a hunch and then make pieces created from the smallest wisps of impulse? And why create so much material, only to discard the vast majority?

First off, improvised, or devised, shows are totally your own. The ensemble or theatre company owns this work and can be proud that they brought a new story into the world. And the material will be personal to the performers, giving them a deep sense of ownership. And finally, most great work comes from trial and error. By chipping away the excess, you're left with a shining jewel.

TRY THIS: IMAGINE GENERATING MATERIAL

- Think about a show you might like to devise.
- What question is at the heart of this story?
- What elements of theatre might uncover this story?
- What kind of movement, music, or language feel the most central to this story?

Can you imagine creating your own improvisations? What kinds of structures could you create to free up performers? What questions might you walk into a rehearsal period with?

WORKSHOPPING THE PRODUCTION

Companies that devise plays often work on a show for months or even years before finishing. They dive into short intense collaborations, spread out by months-long gaps of downtime. Typically, these companies show their work along the way to get feedback, which they use in their next working session. A workshopping process follows a pattern:

- Set a date for a public showing
- String together material to create a draft of the show
- Show to an audience
- Receive feedback
- Go back into rehearsal

This process might repeat several times, with many workshops and public showings. A company might show a thirty-minute "work in progress" for a play that ends up being ninety minutes long. For companies working on a quicker deadline, perhaps they schedule two showings and then a run of a show.

If you're working to devise your first piece, you may only have one shot at a run. Regardless, I encourage you to think about your production as a work in progress. I've seen many students work on a project, only to get such enthusiastic response, they find ways to produce the show again outside of school. Regardless, if you treat this first devising process as a workshop, you take the pressure off yourself to create something perfect.

CREATING A DRAFT

Every company I've read about or interviewed set dates for public showings to create the divine pressure needed for creativity. With infinite time to keep working, they would never commit to making something concrete. The deadline forces them to make decisions.

You start devising a show with a spark, research your topic, and generate material through improvisation. Now what? You gather your songs, games, dances, scenes, and other theatrical moments: what do you do with it all?

If you crave a traditional narrative, look back to the chapter on reading and focus on dramatic structure. Start with a status quo and interrupt with an inciting incident. The hero of the story tries to achieve their dreams, faces obstacles, and hits a turning point. They change their tactics in service of trying to reach the same goal until they hit the climax of the play, followed by a new status quo. Can you string your content together to follow this traditional structure?

The Frantic Assembly theatre structure their works less on narrative and more on visceral pulse. They learned how to shape their pieces by going to clubs and watching DJs work. In speaking to DJs, they learned the science behind the ideal set for dancing. DJs start with a slow beat, something like 120 beats per minute, then slowly build up to a song that was much faster, at say 140 beats per minute. After that climax the DJ would bring the tempo down again. Frantic Assembly uses this kind of structure for their work, building to intense scenes three times in a show, followed by scenes with less intensity.

Frantic Assembly often works with a playwright as part of their devising process. The writer will attend all the movement and choreography workshops, absorbing everything the ensemble generates. They might work off characters actors spawn through improvisation and structure the play around movement pieces the company created. At the end of a workshop the writer creates a first draft linking all the devised material together.

Many companies simply trust their instincts when they want to string work together. If the actors and designers have served as the writers for the piece, now the director can lead the process of culling down to the best material. As a director you can follow your hunches, putting material together that pleases you, creating a repeatable sequence.

Once you have a first draft, now you can start to rehearse in much the same way you rehearse a scripted play. Is there a lot of dialogue? Do you want to do a sit-down table read at this point? Are there new scenes that need staging? Or do you need to create transitions? Are there portions of the play that could benefit from detailed scene work? Do you need to strengthen relationships or actions?

Depending on the scale of support for the production, you'll also need to tech the show in some fashion. Depending on the process you've had, you may have already built in some design moments and now you'll need to bring them together. This is the moment for guiding collaboration between many artists. Let the lighting design have as much narrative power as a character in the play. Trust that a costume moment can hold the audience's attention as much as dialogue. Create moments that delight and surprise.

LISTENING TO THE AUDIENCE

Your devised piece of theatre won't be complete until you have an audience experience the play. I encourage you to have some sort of run through for an invited audience at least a week or two before you open to the public just to learn about what you've made.

Whenever you have the gift of an audience, really listen to them as they watch your show. Just having new ears and eyes in the room will help you see the play differently. Make sure to take note of all the places where the play is working! It's easy to focus on problems, but it's crucial to understand what works. Where did you get laughs? Where was the audience leaning in? Where did they react audibly or visibly to events on stage?

Also, note where the audience tunes out: coughing, rustling, or squirming in seats signal loss of attention. You start to see story points you took for granted because you know the show so well. You discover moments that were clear to you when you broke them down in rehearsal but aren't when the production is flying by at performance speed.

Poll your actors after performances. What felt great and what felt wonky? When did they click with the audience and when did they check out? You don't need to act immediately on this feedback, just store it away to consider later.

SOLICITING AUDIENCE FEEDBACK

A great way to get immediate feedback is to hold a talkback after performances.

If you look back to the last chapter, you'll find advice on setting up and listening to a post-mortem—which is similar to a talkback. If you can, find someone other than yourself to lead the discussion. If you were able to conscript a dramaturg for your project, they would be a great candidate.

As outlined in the last chapter, I recommend following some sort of predetermined feedback structure, perhaps modeled on Liz Lerman's Critical Response Process. A quick review of the order of discussion:

- What did the audience remember? Just images, lines, moments. No judgement.
- What did the audience love about the piece?
- What specific questions do the makers have for the audience?
- What questions do the audience have for the makers?
- Comments from the audience—but only if the makers want to hear them.

For a devised piece, assume you will mostly get comments, questions, and feedback on story, structure, and content. Encourage audiences to give you honest feedback on what they experienced, rather than judgements on what they saw, or recommendations on how to rewrite. You may not be able to avoid unsolicited advice, but encourage people to stick to what they saw, what they felt, and what they understood.

If you've just created a devised piece and received some audience feedback, what do you and your ensemble want to do? Did you learn about the play and now you have a better sense of how to go forward? Can you find another venue to present the piece again? Is there a local new works festival or directors' festival you can apply to? Can you find the space to produce this yourself with your friends?

Before heading back into rehearsal, now is the time to sit down and discuss all the feedback you gathered from audiences and from your own assessment of the performances. Just because many people didn't like one section of the play, is that because it didn't work or because it was in the wrong place? If people loved one type of storyline and say they wanted more, is this what's best for the production?

As you sift through feedback and opinions, a director once again has the key role of finding the signal through the noise.

WHAT DO DIRECTORS DO?

By studying devised theatre, we come back to the original questions about directing. Why is a director necessary? What do they do? What roles do they fill? Why would you want to become a director?

Devised theatre projects typically try to break down hierarchies of all kinds. A lighting designer might have as much say over a moment as a writer or a director or an actor. Actors create dialogue and influence the staging. But a director still leads the production.

A director will typically come to an ensemble with the spark for a show or will lead discussions around possible ideas. In this way they resemble directors who create shows for political or sociological purposes. When they lead warm up exercises, directors start to build ensemble and create a sense of unity in the room. When they offer up prompts for writing and ideas for improvisations, they foster new voices and bring teams of artists together to do their best work. When they start to edit the piece and look for a through line, they help create a theatrical world for the play. When they direct the ensemble and refine the pieces in preparations for showings, they guide, lead, and inspire actors to better performances.

As you go through this book, I hope you imagine yourself as someone who inspires others and works to clarify the vision for a production. When you read through the various stages of production did you find ideas that excite you? As you examine all the different roles a director may fill can you envision yourself in the driver's seat of a production?

Ask yourself: why do I want to direct? And then: start directing!

SUMMARY

In this chapter we focused on the process of devising a piece, or collaboratively writing a play with an ensemble:

- The spark: how to find a motivating theme or question
- Generating material: various ways to structure improvisations
- Workshopping
  - Finding a through line
  - Soliciting audience feedback
  - Going back into rehearsal

FURTHER READING

I highly recommend studying up on theatre games and the two people to start with are Augosto Boal and Viola Spolin. Boal's classics compendium is *Games for Actors and Non-Actors* and Spolin's is *Improvisation for the Theater*. I've drawn heavily from four books in this chapter: *The Viewpoints Book* by Anne Bogart and Tina Laundau, *Moment Work* by Moisés Kaufman and Barbara Pitts McAdams, *The Frantic Assembly Book of Devising Theatre*, and *Ensemble-Made Chicago: A Guide to Devised Theatre* by Chloe Johnston and Coya Paz Brownrigg. There are other books on devising to investigate including *A Beginner's Guide to Devising Theatre* by Jess Thorpe and Tashi Gore.

HELPFUL WEBSITES

I encourage you to check out the websites of companies that devise theatre
including these:
www.siti.org
www.tectonictheaterproject.org
www.theteamplays.org
www.franticassembly.co.uk
www.aboutfacetheatre.com
www.pigpentheatre.com

WORKBOOK

READING

1. THE FIRST READ

Turn off all your phones and shut off all electronic devices. Make yourself comfortable.

Read the first act of a play trying to experience it as an audience member. If there's an intermission, take a break. Stand up and walk around. How has the play affected you so far? Read the second act without a break.

Write down general reactions. Don't worry too much about the writing—just jot down what comes to you. Were you engaged? Did it affect you emotionally? Do you have questions?

Keep these answers close to you as you work your way through the process. Your first impressions guide developing a point of view (pp. 41–44), answering six questions (pp. 41–44), creating an outline for a first design meeting (pp. 52–54), and writing a first day address (pp. 82–83).

2. GIVEN CIRCUMSTANCES

A given circumstance is a fact discovered in the script. It's not a matter of opinion.

Start reading from the beginning of the play and on one piece of paper write down any facts about events that happened before the play

DOI: 10.4324/9781003016922-8

began or places that exist. On another piece write down questions. Now take your list of facts and organize them into useful categories.

Make a list of given circumstances about every room, building, and place mentioned in the play. If you like, sketch out some pictures or ground plans based on what you found.

Organize the given circumstances for each character in chronological order. Combine this with dramaturgical work to create a biographical sketch.

Now turn to your questions and see which ones you can answer before rehearsal begins through research and close re-reading.

Believing in given circumstances form the basis for great acting according to Stanislavski (10). These given circumstances help you create character breakdowns (pp. 67–69) and lead effective design meetings (pp. 62–65). Knowing the facts of the script form the bedrock of effective direction when delving into scene work (pp. 99–101).

3. FRENCH SCENES

To break your play into French scenes, mark a division every time someone enters or exits. Create a table to organize the information about how long the French scene lasts in pages, and who is in the scene.

French scenes are one of the many ways we mark action and change in a play (pp. 35–36). Examine the pattern created and see what you learn about the play's structure. See Appendix 3 for a French scene breakdown for A Raisin in the Sun.

4. EVENTS

An event is a moment where a change happens that affects everyone on stage. Every entrance and exit marks an event. A change in the topic of conversation doesn't mark an event, but a big shift in action does.

Go through the play and identify each event. Name each event as simply as possible.

Plays are made from action in the same way that paintings are made of oils and canvas. It's what happens on stage that creates story, plot, and suspense (pp. 36–37).

5. DRAMATIC ANALYSIS

Survey the entire play and chart the dramatic structure. How does the main character's fortune rise and fall?

- **Who is the protagonist?** *Whose journey are we following?*
- **What is the protagonist's spine?** *What is the main thing they are trying to do?*
- **Who is the antagonist?** *Who opposes the protagonist?*
- **What is the antagonist's spine?** *Are the antagonist and protagonist in conflict?*
- **What is the status quo or stasis?** *As the play begins what is the unchanging situation?*
- **What is the inciting incident?** *What happens to the protagonist to upset the status quo?*
- **What is the dramatic question?** *What question are we tracking?*
- **What is the rising action?** *How does the protagonist try to achieve their goal?*
- **What is the turning point?** *What forces the protagonist to change their attack?*
- **Falling Action** *After the turning point how does the protagonist try to achieve their dream?*
- **Climax** *Does the protagonist achieve their goal?*
- **New Status Quo** *What is the new unchanging situation?*

The main character's journey through the play can help track moments of suspense, change in direction, and momentum. Knowing how the script is structured may help you understand why the play affects you emotionally (pp. 37–40).

DESIGNING

6. THE SIX QUESTIONS

Look over your first read notes, dramatic analysis, and given circumstances. Now answer these six key questions.

- What is the play about?
- What kind of play is it?

- What is the dramatic question of the play?
- What is the spine of the play?
- What do you want to do to the audience?
- What is the cry of the play?

Remember, you can re-evaluate or even change these answers later. Trust your instincts now. You can use the answers to develop a point of view to bring into a first design meeting (pp. 41–44).

7. PREPARE FOR A FIRST DESIGN MEETING

A you prepare to discuss the set, lights, costumes, and sound for the show, be prepared with the following:

- Point of view on the play
- Simple story of the play
- Understanding of the opportunities and challenges the script present: what kind of theatre are we in and what kind of design does the play call for?
- Clear guidelines on the scope of the production: budget, time and level of support

Now remember, when you go into the meeting that it's as important for you to hear from your designers as for you to express your point of view. Try to practice generous listening and flexibility. (pp. 52–58)

8. THE MOMENT CHAIN

Make a list of about twenty-four important moments (eighteen for a ninety-minute one act). These moments should be able to tell the narrative and emotional story of the play. Pick events, lines, pauses—rather than entire scenes.

You can use this moment chain to check the progress of your design. Do you have costume, sound, set, and light ideas to support some of these important events? Look at your ground plan, do you have a variety of places to stage each of these key moments (pp. 63–64)? See Appendix 4 for a moment chain for The Seagull.

CASTING

9. WRITE UP CHARACTER BREAKDOWNS

For each character in the play write a short paragraph describing the role to prepare for casting.

- What are the basics about age, race, ethnicity, gender, and role?
- What is the one thing this character needs to do that you cannot teach?
- What big action does the character perform in the play?

Remember that you are trying to be specific enough to help choose potential actors to come in for auditions, but open enough to be surprised during callbacks (pp. 67–69).

10. CHOOSE SIDES FOR AUDITIONS

For each major character, choose two audition sides. You want to pick scenes that are about two pages in length, without any major intimacy, violence, or hard to complete action.

- Pick two contrasting scenes, one showing a lighter side to the character.
- Pick a side that shows you the key quality you're looking for in the actor.
- Pick sides that you look forward to hearing many times over.

Picking sides helps you decide what is important about this character. What must you see them do before you go into rehearsal? What is the essence of this character (pp. 70–72)?

REHEARSING

11. PLANNING YOUR TIME

Look at the amount of time the theatre has given you. Examine your play. How will you get from the first rehearsal in the room to the first technical rehearsal?

- Are there special circumstances in your play that will take extra time? When do you want to work on them? How long will they take? For example:
  - Music
  - Dance
  - Fights
  - Intimacy
  - Large crowd scenes
- Does your play have complicated language? Do you want to unravel the intricacies up front or as you go?
- Do you want to build slowly or make a few passes through the play?
- When are designer run-throughs? How many does the theatre require?
- How much of the play can you discover in the rehearsal room and what will you need to leave for tech?
- Where can you build-in flexibility?

Make a draft with your stage management team. Show it to a producer or an assistant director—did you leave anything out? (See Appendix 4 for a Sample Rehearsal Schedule.)

12. OPENING DAY SPEECH

Write out a speech to give on the first day of rehearsal. Be sure to tell the story from your point of view. Inspire your collaborators. Why this play? Why now? Why this team of artists?

Read out loud to a fellow student or a teacher. What resonated for them? What fell flat? Revise and repeat.

While you may end up improvising your speech or speaking from notes in rehearsal, you'll clarify your thoughts if you write them down. Clear writing comes from clear thinking. This is a chance to summarize everything you feel about the play and why it's worth doing (pp. 82–83).

13. SOME QUESTIONS TO ASK DURING TABLE WORK

Almost any question can bear fruit during table work. Here are some basic ones to stir discussion:

- Who's in the scene? What's their relationship? How long have they known each other?
- Where are we? What's here? Why are we here?
- How is this scene different from the last one we read?
- What is the most important event in the scene?
- What's the basic situation? Is someone coming soon? Or leaving soon? Are we preparing for something? Dealing with new information?
- Why do they speak? Why do they listen?
- Do you understand the language? Do you notice anything from the way the scene is written?

You can't ask all these questions of every scene; follow your instincts about what will spur discussion. Let curiosity guide the room. I encourage you to read in sections rather than interrupting actors; maybe read French scenes and discuss (pp. 85–86).

14. CHARACTER WEBS

Ask your actors to describe the current state of their relationship with every other character.

Name the literal relationship: son, mother, former lover, teacher. Describe why they love the other person. What drives them crazy? What past common experiences do they share? What problem are they trying to solve with the other person?

You may use these character webs in several ways:

- Discuss as a group
- Discuss one-on-one with each actor
- Create a group craft project
- Fashion a movement exercise
- Let the actors keep their results a complete secret

The more actors in the cast, the more lines between characters, and the more complicated the web of relationships becomes. You might use this work when you're building the world or when you are delving into scene work.

15. RUNNING WITH NO REHEARSAL

This exercise works best if you surprise the cast.

Either in the afternoon after finishing up table work, or at the top of day, announce that you'll be running the play from top to bottom. Set up a few guidelines so the ensemble can run without stopping, figuring out challenges in the moment:

- If there's any intimacy, tell the actors to hug each other or make eye contact.
- If there's violence, simulate the fight without touching.
- No speaking except for lines from the play.
- Actors may enter and exit from anywhere.
- Indicate a general playing space.
- People may bring on simple furniture and props or mime the essentials.
- Have Fun!

Typically, some folks will be confused, others excited, and a few completely terrified. I encourage you to rip off the Band-Aid and say: "Okay, let's go!" (pp. 90–91).

16. PREPARING FOR STAGING

Before working on a scene for the first time, ask yourself questions about the structure and purpose of the section:

- Who's in the scene?
- Where are they? When does the scene take place?
- When did they last see each other?
- If they are entering—where from?
- If they exit—where to?
- If they start on stage—how long have they been there? Doing what?
- What's the tone? How is it different from the scene before and after?
- Where does this scene take place in the arc of the play?
- Where are the major events or beat shifts?

- How is the beginning of the scene different than the end?
- Do you have clear images or hunches about how people relate to each other and the space physically?
- Does the dialogue of the scene indicate any specific physical business or behavior?
- Have you investigated the author's stage directions?

Read the scene over once or twice. Try to visualize it but leave space for new choices the actors will bring. These basic questions can guide you as you start to create staging with your cast, delve deeper into the scene work, and as you observe run-throughs and try to give notes. Keep these lists at hand for each scene to diagnose problems and celebrate successes.

17. SOME QUESTIONS TO ASK YOUR STAGING

Ask these questions as you prepare to stage the play, after your first sketch, and before heading into technical rehearsals.

- Have you used every part of the stage or are you stuck center stage too often?
- If you turned the sound off on your play, could you understand it?
  - Would you recognize relationships?
  - Does status come across?
  - Do you know where you are?
  - Does the story progress physically as well as emotionally?
- Have you placed each scene in the most effective part of the stage?
- Have you highlighted the most important moments?
- Are you spending too much time on non-essential business?
- Do you recognize your staging as truthful?
- Have you created beauty? Metaphor?
- Can you simplify?

Give this list to a dramaturg or assistant director. Embolden them to check your work. If someone is coming to give notes, you might ask them questions about what they saw (pp. 114–117).

18. COACHING ACTORS

As you delve into the details of scene work, here are some questions to ask your actors:

- What is the current state of your relationships?
- What do you want from the other person? What obstacle stands in your way? What does winning look like? What will it cost you if you lose?
- What's the time of day? Season? Time of year?
- How are you affected by this space? Is it a place you know?
- What's happened in the last twenty-four hours?
- What are the key given circumstances that affect the scene?
- Where are the key decision points in the scene?
- Are you carrying any secrets?
- Are there opportunities for humor?

Read the scene with these questions in mind. You may want to keep a list of key given circumstances at hand (pp. 96–103).

19. TROUBLESHOOTING SCENES

You view a scene. You know it's not working. What can you do? Here's a list of questions:

- Should you try changing where characters enter from? What about the exit?
- Are the status roles clear? Do they change?
- What happening at the beginning of the scene? The end? Are they different?
- Is the pace off? Are people rushing their decisions? Or slowing down where they should be driving?
- Is every moment of the scene given the same weight? How can you find variety?
- Is the scene playing the same as the scene before or after?
- Are the actors playing for emotion rather than action?
- Do the actors understand what they are saying and why?
- Do they need some sort of physical business?

Don't be afraid to use the same tools over and over. Or to surprise yourself with new diagnostic techniques. Feel free to tell your cast that you think something is off in the scene but you're not sure what, maybe they will have an answer. These lists can also guide you as you watch run-throughs and give notes (pp. 118–120).

20. DIRECTING TRANSITIONS

A transition transports the audience from one scene to the next. During technical rehearsals you spend much of your time working with sound and lighting designers to finesse these moments of change. As you watch, think through these checklists.

- Is the final moment of the first scene clear to the audience, do you need to hold on it a moment longer to land what just happened?
- What starts the transition? Does sound and light lead, or is it the movement of an actor?
- Are lights and sound working together?
- Is there a story to be told in the transition?
- Do we know where to look during the transition?
- Does everyone on stage know what they are doing? Do they understand their cues?
- When you start the next scene is the situation clear from the top? Do we know where we are and what is happening?

Remember that in technical rehearsals your key roles are storyteller, time manager, and group leader. As you watch these transitions try to track the story of the entire play as well as this specific moment. Don't micromanage your designers but instead guide them and listen to their ideas. Rather than obsessing over every detail, can you create a general structure for the transition and move on, checking it again during a run-through?

OPENING

21. LISTENING TO A POSTMORTEM

After your production is over, can you gather some friends and fellow students to talk about the production? Can you have someone you trust lead this discussion? Follow this method for the discussion and try to keep folks from telling you how to re-direct the play.

- What do they remember?
- What did they love about the show?
- What questions do you have for them?
- What questions do they have for you?
- Do they have any burning comments?

In terms of questions to ask you could see what story people took away from the show or perhaps how design helped or hindered the production. Perhaps you want to know about specific relationships and how they played out. Remember that the most important critique is your own (pp. 126–128).

Appendix 1
SUMMARY OF *THE SEAGULL*
BY ANTON CHEKHOV

ACT 1

A young man, Constantine, prepares to present a new play he wrote starring his girlfriend, Nina. He erected a makeshift stage on his uncle Sorin's estate, and the audience includes his famous actress mother, Arkadina, and her boyfriend, the well-known writer, Trigorin. As the play begins, Arkadina starts making little jokes about the oddness of the production. After trying to shush her several times, Constantine stops the show and storms off. Masha, daughter of the estate manager, Shamrayev, runs off to try to fetch Constantine. Everyone retires to the house except Dorn, a local doctor who says he really liked the play. Constantine returns, and Masha rushes in telling him to see his mother, but he refuses and storms off again. Masha confesses to Dorn that she's in love with Constantine.

ACT 2

People laze about the estate in the hot sun including Sorin, who's health seems to be worse. Shamrayev comes to ask Arkadina if she planned to go to town with his wife Paulina. When Arkadina says she had, a huge fight erupts about what horses she might use and everyone storms off, Arkadina vowing to leave the estate. Nina is left alone when Constantine comes in and lays a dead seagull at her feet. He starts to complain that Nina no longer loves him, but just then Trigorin arrives and Constantine retreats. When Nina says she wishes she could be famous like him, Trigorin goes on a long tirade saying he finds being a well-known writer tortuous. Nina says he just works too hard and should appreciate what he has. Arkadina comes back and through tears tells Trigorin they are staying after all.

ACT 3

One week later, Arkadina and Trigorin are packing to leave because apparently Constantine shot himself. Nina gives Trigorin a medallion with an engraving that lists the title of one of his books and a page and line number. Sorin and Arkadina argue over whether she could afford to give her son some money, and Sorin has a bit of an attack. When he goes to lie down, Constantine asks Arkadina to change his bandage. At first mother and son seem to be reconciled, but soon get into a shouting match over Trigorin. Just as they make up again, Trigorin enters with his book and Constantine escapes. Trigorin finds the line referenced on the medallion which reads, "If you should ever need my life, it is yours for the asking." In a passionate fit he asks Arkadina to release him so he can pursue Nina. She refuses him and wins him back with a passionate speech. Everyone gathers to see Arkadina and Trigorin off, but just as they exit, Trigorin comes back in. He sees Nina and they plan to meet up in Moscow, ending the act with a long kiss.

ACT 4

Two years later Sorin is dying and his sister and Trigorin are coming to visit after a long time away. Doctor Dorn arrives back from a long trip and asks about Nina. Constantine tells a sad tale: Nina ran away with Trigorin, had a child which died, he left her, and she's struggling to make a life as an actor. When Trigorin arrives with Arkadina, everyone makes awkward conversation for a bit until retiring for dinner. In a surprise, Nina shows up to see Constantine. She's very hungry and cold and seems slightly manic, referring to herself as a seagull. Constantine declares his love for her, but she claims to still love Trigorin. She recites a bit of Constantine's play from two years ago and flees into the night. Constantine rips up all his manuscripts and exits. Everyone comes back to the room to continue the party when a muffled shot is heard. Dorn goes to investigate, returning to say all is well. But in a twist, he pulls Trigorin aside to tell him to get Arkadina out of the room because Constantine shot himself. The play ends abruptly.

Appendix 2
SUMMARY OF *A RAISIN IN THE SUN* BY LORRAINE HANSBERRY

ACT 1

At the top of the play, the Youngers, a three-generation Black family, all live cramped into a small apartment on Chicago's South side. They are eagerly awaiting a $10,000 life insurance check which is coming due to the death of Mama's husband. Her son, Walter Lee, is struggling to make it as a limousine driver and tries to get his wife, Ruth, excited about a plan to spend the money on a liquor store. Beneatha, Walter's sister, reminds him that it's up to Mama how to spend the money, and she hopes to use some to pay for medical school. Mama thinks it would be nice to put a down payment on a small house with a yard for Travis, Walter and Ruth's son. Mama tells Walter repeatedly she doesn't like the idea of selling liquor, which she believes is sinful. When Mama discovers that Ruth is pregnant and considering getting an abortion, she confronts Walter, but he leaves the house saying no one understands him.

ACT 2

Walter tries to get his family to listen to him about his plans to make something of himself. He and Ruth have trouble connecting. Mama comes home to say she put a down payment on a house in a white neighborhood, Clybourne Park, because it was the only one she could afford. Walter says she's just killed his dream. To bolster Walter, Mama says she only spent $3500 of the $10,000 and gives the rest to Walter. She tells him to put $3000 in the bank for Beneatha's tuition, and the rest Walter can spend as the head of the family. Walter has an emotional moment with his son where he says he's going to make a business transaction that will start them on the road to riches.

ACT 3

It's moving day for the Youngers but their packing is interrupted by a white man, Mr. Lindner, a representative from the Clybourne Park Improvement association. Lindner tells Walter and Beneatha and Ruth that the association doesn't think it's a good idea for a Black family to move into a white neighborhood and is prepared to buy them out at a profit. Walter tells Lindner to get out of his house. Walter's friend Bobo arrives, and we discover that Walter didn't put any money in the bank, but instead gave it all to their mutual friend Willy who was supposed to help them get a liquor license. But Willy has stolen the money and taken off.

Walter tells everyone that he's decided to call Lindner back and accept his offer and take the money to not move to Clybourne Park. Mama and Beneatha tell Walter that he'll feel ashamed for taking that deal. When Lindner shows up Walter tries to send his son Travis away, but Mama says no, Travis should stay and see what kind of man his father is. In that moment, Walter makes a decision. He turns to Lindner and says that his family is full of proud people and that he cannot accept their offer. He shows Lindner the door and the family giddily prepares to move out to Clybourne park and their new home.

Appendix 3
FRENCH SCENES CHART

A Raisin in the Sun

ACT 1

Scene	1.1	1.2	1.3	1.4	1.5	1.6	1.7	1.8	1.9	2.1	2.2	2.3	2.4	2.5	2.6	2.7	2.8	2.9	2.10	2.11
Pages	1	1–2	2–3	3–4	4–5	5–6	6–8	8–11	11–14	14	14	14–15	15–16	16–17	17–18	18	18	18	18	19–21
Ruth	X	X	X	X	X	X	X	X	X				X			X	X	X	X	X
Travis	X	X	X												X			X	X	
Walter		X			X	X				X										X
Beneatha							X	X		X	X	X	X	X	X	X	X	X		X
Mama								X	X	X	X	X	X	X	X	X	X	X	X	X
Asagai														X	X					

ACT 2

Scene	1.1	1.2	1.3	1.4	1.5	1.6	1.7	1.8	1.9	2.1	2.2	2.3	2.4	2.5	2.6	2.7
Pages	21	21–22	22	22–23	23	23–24	25	25–27	27–29	29–30	30	30	30	30–31	31	31–32
Ruth	X	X	X	X	X	X	X	X	X				X	X		
Travis															X	X
Walter		X	X			X	X			X	X	X			X	X
Beneatha	X	X	X	X					X	X				X	X	X
Mama											X	X	X			
Asagai																
George			X		X	X			X	X	X					

ACT 2 (CONT.)

Scene	3.1	3.2	3.3	3.4	3.5
Pages	33–34	34–36	36–38	39–40	40
Ruth	X	X	X	X	X
Travis			X	X	X
Walter	X	X	X	X	X
Beneatha	X	X	X	X	X
Mama			X	X	X
Asagai					
George		X			
Lindner					
Bobo				X	

ACT 3

Scene	1.1	1.2	1.3	1.4	1.5	1.6	1.7
Pages	41–44	44	44–45	45–47	48	47–48	48–49
Ruth		X	X	X	X	X	X
Travis					X	X	X
Walter				X	X	X	X
Beneatha	X	X	X	X	X	X	X
Mama			X	X	X	X	X
Asagai	X						
George							
Lindner						X	
Bobo							

Appendix 4
MOMENT CHAIN FOR *THE SEAGULL* BY ANTON CHEKHOV

1. Constantine tells Sorin "There's a real stage for you"—showing off the set for his play.
2. Nina and Constantine kiss.
3. The curtain is pulled, Nina is revealed, and the play begins.
4. Constantine stops the play yelling at Arkadina.
5. Everyone stops for a moment and listens to singing across the lake.
6. Masha confesses to Dorn that she is in love with Constantine.
7. Sorin's loud snore interrupts Masha's rapturous talk about Constantine.
8. Masha limps off away from her friends—clearly hiding that she is drunk.
9. Shamrayev, Arkadina, Nina, Medvedenko, and Sorin storm out after fighting.
10. Paulina rips up a flower Nina gave to Dorn.
11. Constantine puts a dead seagull at Nina's feet.
12. Trigorin tells Nina his idea for a short story subject in which a man meets a girl like her and destroys her out of pure boredom.
13. Nina gives Trigorin a medallion and asks him to see her for two minutes before he leaves.

14. Sorin collapses and Arkadina calls for help.
15. Arkadina screams at Constantine calling him a failure, and he collapses in tears.
16. Trigorin asks Arkadina to release him so he can pursue Nina.
17. Arkadina says "now I have him" after getting Trigorin to give up on Nina.
18. Long kiss between Trigorin and Nina.
19. Masha waltzes alone to Constantine playing the piano offstage.
20. Sorin says that if they send for his sister, he must really be sick, and the room falls silent.
21. Constantine notices that Trigorin didn't read his stories in a literary magazine.
22. Constantine pulls Nina into the room.
23. Constantine rips up all his manuscripts.
24. Dorn tells Trigorin that Constantine shot himself.

Appendix 5
SAMPLE REHEARSAL SCHEDULE

SUNDAY	MONDAY	TUESDAY	WEDNESDAY	THURSDAY	FRIDAY	SATURDAY
		May 1 First rehearsal Meet and greet	**2** Table work Dance/Fights	**3** Table work Dance/Fights	**4** Table work Dance/Fight	**5** Surprise Run through! Start Staging
6 Continue Staging	**7** Day Off	**8** Continue Staging	**9** Continue Staging	**10** Run First act Review Dance/Fights	**11** Continue Staging	**12** Continue Staging
13 Review dance/fights **First Run**	**14** Day Off	**15** Detailed scene work	**16** Detailed scene work	**17** Review dance/fights Run First act	**18** Detailed scene work	**19** Detailed Scene work
20 Review dance/fights **Designer Run**	**21** Day Off	**22** Work Run Act 1	**23** Work Run Act 2	**24** Work Final Run	**25** Work in theatre space	**26** Tech
27 Tech	**28** Day Off	**29** Tech Dress Run	**30** First Preview	**31** Work time 2nd Preview	**June 1** Work Time 3rd Preview	**2** Work time 4th Preview
3 5th Preview	**4** Day Off	**5** Tech Day	**6** Work 6th Preview	**7** Work 7th Preview	**8** **Opening Night!**	

SAMPLE REHEARSAL SCHEDULE

This rehearsal schedule moves from first rehearsal to opening night in just about a month and is predicated on many assumptions:

- I imagined a set of fights and dances that could be worked in the first week and then reviewed in the weeks after. I chose fights and dances but this could be time for dialect work, singing, specific movement exercises, intimacy, etc.
- I assumed the director wanted a few days of table work in the beginning.
- I threw in a surprise run through!
- I assumed the theatre wanted a designer run through a week before tech.
- I gave a lot of time for previews and work during previews—this is quite generous. Many theatres would open by June 2 or 3 without a second week of work. I have found that on new plays especially, this second week is invaluable.

This is only one model of rehearsal and I purposely didn't put in rehearsal hours as either the union contract, university policies, or theatre policies will dictate when and how long you can rehearse.

Appendix 6
KIMBERLY SENIOR'S LIST OF RUN-THROUGH TARGETS

AN EDITED SELECTION

- No judgment of your own character
- Activate the language
- Love your scene partner
- Find access to joy
- Connect the dots of thought for your character
- Who has the status in every moment of the play?
- Who is your line intended for?
- Simplify
- Play to win
- Spend it all—to raise the stakes
- Defend your ideals
- Precision of beats and language
- Pay attention to details
- Today is the day
- Find the opposites (both within your character and in your intentions)
- Generosity: share the play with the audience
- Stay on task no matter what
- Seek the obstacles

- Keep your secrets
- Use the right tool for the job
- When in doubt, choose love
- Be the best attorney for your character
- Surprise your scene partner
- Form alliances
- Aggressive listening: find your next line in what just happened on stage
- 360 degree awareness: emotionally and physically
- Whose play is it? *Your* play. Place yourself at the center of the story.
- Find the danger
- The last scene of the play is the first of the next
- What do you drive into the scene with? What's the detour?
- Lean into the discomfort
- Hold on to optimism as long as you can
- Efficiency, economy of language, action, movement
- Crave intimacy

GLOSSARY

Action When faced with an obstacle, what an actor does to get what they want. Action may be expressed through dialogue, physical business, or emotional manipulation. Action can be charted in a map of sorts by plotting the biggest decisions or crises in the play, as well as the main actions of the lead character.

Actor–Manager The leader of a theatrical company who acts in the starring role of plays, while also organizing the business of the company.

Alienation Effect A technique, popularized by German director Bertolt Brecht, in which audience members are purposely distanced from the scene they are viewing with the goal that they will think critically about what they are watching.

Beat The smallest unit of dramatic action in a script. In a beat, characters pursue a simple action. If they change actions as the result of conflict, a new beat has begun.

Blocking A term from the 19th century when directors used a model of the set and colored blocks to stand in for actors. They would then plan out all the movements of the characters and come to rehearsal to teach the actors their blocking.

Channel Work Work an actor does to create creating a specific relationship with every other character in the play.

Character Breakdown A short description of a character used for directors and casting directors to create lists of actors for auditions for a play. Should cover basics such as age, race, gender (if appropriate) as well as a description of how they behave and what they do.

Climax   When the dramatic tension and conflict from throughout the play come to a head. When the protagonist makes the final big decision in the play and the dramatic question that was asked at the inciting incident is answered.

Composition Work   Seen as a companion to Viewpoints Training, actors are asked to complete a complicated set of tasks in a short amount of time. The goal is to work quickly, collaboratively, and without judgment to create short theatrical pieces.

Concepts Meeting   A design meeting where designers will show their initial research and share first ideas about where they are heading.

Conflict   Tension between two characters because of opposing actions or desires. One character wants something, and another wants the opposite.

Critical Response Process   A way for artists to receive feedback on their work developed by choreographer Liz Lerman. A facilitator leads the audience through a group of specific prompts, helping the artists receive the feedback they really crave.

Design Meeting   A meeting where all the designers on a production, led by the director discuss how they will realize the sets, lights, costumes, sound, and any other technical aspects. Design meetings are often collaborative, discursive, and focused on the art of the show. (See Production Meetings)

Devising   A process where an ensemble starts rehearsal without a set script and through different types of improvisations creates a play collaboratively. Also known as company creation.

Dramatic Pyramid   A tool for analyzing dramatic action created by Gustav Freytag in the mid-1800s. The play starts with the status quo that is interrupted by the inciting incident, which leads to a rising tension as the hero pursues their goal. The action changes at the turning point of the play, hurtling toward the climax of the play, followed by a new status quo.

Dramatic Question   What is in suspense throughout the play. Typically, about the protagonist and their quest that was kicked off at the inciting incident.

Dramaturg   A person working on a play who's focused on the dramaturgy, or theatre specific story telling aspects of the play. For existing plays, dramaturgs often will conduct research on the time period or the playwright. For new plays, dramaturgs serve as editors of sorts, acting as the play's representative in productions.

Dramaturgy The study of crafting a story into a theatrical form. Dramaturgy is concerned with all aspects of a play including context, structure, language, and theatricality. Dramaturgy is concerned with understanding the language of theatre as opposed to that of film, novels, or other artforms.

Empathy When an audience member identifies with and feels for a character. They are swept into the story, forget they are watching a play, and begin to feel what the character is feeling.

Event A change that affects everyone on stage. Every entrance and exit marks an event. An event causes change on stage and often comes as the result of a decision by a character.

Falling Action What the protagonist tries to do in the second half of a play to achieve their dreams and get what they want. After the turning point and before the climax.

Fantastic Realism A concept invented by Yevgeny Vakhtangov, a star director in Russia in the early 20th Century, in which actors play scenes truthfully according to the imaginary given circumstances the ensemble invents.

First Day Address A short speech made by the director on the first day of rehearsal, usually in front of the entire cast and design team designed to orient the company in a direction.

French Scene A unit of dramatic action without any exits or entrances. Every time someone enters or exits the stage, this marks a new French Scene.

Generating Material A part of the devising process where ensemble members create theatrical material that will make up the eventual show.

Given Circumstances The facts of a play that actors and directors use to create grounded performances. These facts include events from the past, places that exists, as well as historical research.

Greek Poet Also known as the didaskalos, or teacher, they wrote the Greek tragedies and satyr plays that played at the Festival of Dionysus in the 5th century B.C.E.

Improvisation An exercise where actors make up dialogue and/
or action based on a clear set of rules. A leader sets out expectations and often guides the actors as they play out a scenario.

Inciting Incident The moment something happens to the protagonist of the play which sparks the dramatic conflict. The dramatic question is asked at this moment.

Magic If Invented by Stanislavski, one of the key methods for creating truthful acting. An actor imagines they are in the situation
of a character in a play and then acts accordingly. The actor asks
themselves the question, "If I faced these given circumstances
what would I do?"

Moment Chain An analytical tool created by Jon Jory in which
directors list the 24 most important moments in the play. If you
saw these moments, you would receive the narrative and emotional heart of the play.

Moment Work A process for devising theater created by the
Tectonic Theater Project. Ensemble members work with theatrical tools to create short repeatable pieces. These theatrical
tools can include lights, props, sound, music, text, movement,
and anything else that speaks on stage.

New Play Workshop A forum where a writer comes together
with actors, directors, and dramaturgs to work on their script.
Typically, they will hear their play out loud, discuss, and potentially make changes. There is often some sort of presentation
at the end of the working period, with actors holding scripts,
sometimes standing at music stands.

New Status Quo After the climax, the new unchanging situation,
marked by a lack of dramatic conflict.

Pageant Manager The organizer of Medieval Mystery plays that
depicted popular bible stories, often outdoors in town squares.
They hired stage manager to oversee the acting, special effects,
crowds, and construction of sets and props.

Point of View A director's vision for a play, based on how they
view the story. The point of view is based on what parts of the
play they plan to heighten, and how they hope the show reso-
nates for an audience.

Poor Theatre A movement created by Polish director Jerzy
Grotowski that sought to create theatre with the least amount

of materials. Shows would be created without special lighting, limited props and set, very simple costumes, no sound cues, and very little in the way between actor and audience.

Postmortem Postmortem comes from the Latin and literally means, after death. In the theatre, the postmortem is a chance to evaluate the entire production with the benefit of hindsight.

Previews Performances for an audience before the official opening, when the director, actors, and designers are still working.

Production Meeting A meeting that includes all the designers, as well as all the production and technical people on the show. Production meetings are typically meant to be focused on issues that need to be discussed between departments and will cover technical details. These meetings are often focused, move department by department, and specific. (See Design Meetings.)

Relationship How one character views another character, leading to how they interact with them. Should contain elements of love and conflict. Relationships are deepened by shared histories, past events, relative status, roles, and how they talk about each other.

Rising Action What the protagonist tries to do in the first half of a play to achieve their dreams and get what they want. What they do between the inciting incident and the turning point.

Run-through When the cast starts at the beginning of the play and performs it until the end without stopping except for intermission breaks.

Scene Work Rehearsal time spent trying to uncover hidden meaning, develop character, create dramatic tension, unlock events, and improve the playing of scenes of a play. This work will involve crafting moments, creating staging, working on given circumstances, creating conflict, and developing actions.

Side A short scenes used for auditions. Typically, two to three pages, running three to five minutes in length. Pulled by a director or casting director and provided to actors to prepare.

Spect-Actor In the theatre of Augosto Boal, when audience members are encouraged to leave their seats and take part in the action on stage.

Stage Directions Instructions in the script that define staging and settings and sometimes character description and motivation. Some stage directions are written by the playwright and others may have been put in by the publisher.

Staging A repeatable set of movements that the actors will do every night. This movement is created in rehearsals, typically in a collaboration between the director and the actors. The staging is recorded by the stage manager in their prompt book so that there is a reference.

Stakes Why the outcome of a dramatic conflict matters to each of the characters. Stakes typically want to be raised in a scene which can be done when the actors care more about the outcome.

Status Quo The unchanging state of affairs at the top of a play, marked by a lack of dramatic conflict. Interrupted by the inciting incident.

Table Work An initial period in rehearsal where actors read sections of the play while sitting around the table, asking questions, clarifying ideas, and discussing the script. This can last a few days to more than a week and prepares actors for staging rehearsals.

Talkback Like a postmortem, a guided discussion designed to help artists get feedback on what an audience took away from a performance. These usually happen right after a showing and are best when specifically led by a facilitator.

Technical Rehearsals Often shortened to "tech," when all the lighting, sound, projection, and other technical cues are rehearsed with the actors, stage manager, and designers. The exact timing for each cue is rehearsed, as well as the levels of the lighting and sound. Any transitions between scenes, props, and costume changes are also rehearsed.

Turning Point What happens to the protagonist at the mid-point of a play to make them change course, usually to a more dangerous and desperate course of action to get what they want.

Twelve Guideposts Created by Michael Shurtleff, twelve ways to look at an audition side to improve performances. The guideposts: Relationship, fighting for, moment before, humor, opposites, discoveries, communication and competition, importance, events, place, game playing and role playing, mystery and secret.

Viewpoints Training   A method of actor or dance training where participants learn to improvise physically, emphasizing certain modalities or Viewpoints. Some of the Viewpoints include: Space, Kinesthetic Response, Gesture, Architecture, Tempo, Duration, Topography, and Repetition.

Workshopping   A process whereby a company sets a deadline for a showing, performs material for an audience, receives feedback, and then goes back into rehearsal for revisions. This process can last anywhere from weeks to years and can involve many iterations of the showing and revising process.

World Building   A preparatory time at the beginning of rehearsal where actors learn about the rules of the play: how language works, how characters move, what rules govern behavior. This world building may come from table work, physical exercises, games, and delving into play specific dramaturgy.

World of the Play   A fictional universe that may resemble our own world but is specific to the script of a play. The world is created by how time, space, language, power, sound, music, and other qualities act in this specific world.

BIBLIOGRAPHY

Aristotle. *Poetics*. Translated by Malcolm Heath. London: Penguin Books, 1996.

Artaud, Antonin. *The Theatre and Its Double*. New York, NY: Grove Press, 1958.

Bartow, Arthur. *The Director's Voice: Twenty-one Interviews*. New York, NY: Theatre Communications Group, 1988.

Ball, David. *Backwards and Forwards: A Technical Manual for Reading Plays*. Carbondale: Southern Illinois University Press, 1983.

Ball, William. *A Sense of Direction*. Hollywood, CA: Quite Specific Media Group Ltd., 1984.

Benedetti, Jean. *Stanislavski: A Life*. New York, NY: Methuen, 1999.

Benedetti, Jean. *Stanislavski and the Actor*. New York, NY: Routledge, 1998.

Benedetti, Jean. *Stanislavski in Rehearsal*. New York, NY: Methuen Drama, 2014.

Bloom, Michael. *Thinking Like a Director: A Practical Handbook*. New York, NY: Faber and Faber, 2001.

Boal, Augusto. *Games for Actors and Non-Actors*. Translated by Adrian Jackson. New York, NY: Routledge, 1992.

Boal, Augusto. *Theatre of the Oppressed*. Translated by Charles A. McBride. New York, NY: Theatre Communications Group, 1985.

Bogart, Anne. *A Director Prepares: Seven Essays on Art and Theatre*. New York, NY: Routledge, 2001.

Bogart, Anne and Tina Landau. *The Viewpoints Book: A Practical Guide to Viewpoints and Composition*. New York, NY: Theatre Communications Group, 2005.

Brecht, Bertolt. *Brecht on Brecht: The Development of an Aesthetic*. Translated by John Willett. New York, NY: Hill & Wang, 1994.

Brook, Peter. *The Empty Space*. New York: Touchstone, 1968.

brown, adrienne maree. *Emergent Strategy: Shaping Change, Changing Worlds*. Chico, CA: AK Press, 2017.

Brown, John Russell. "Shakespeare and the Natyasastra," *Shakespeare in Asia*. Cambridge: Cambridge University Press, 2010.

Carnicke, Sharon Marie. *Stanislavsky in Focus: An Acting Master for the Twenty-first Century*. Oxon: Routledge, 1998. Reprint: Routledge, 2009.

Chekhov, Anton. *A Life in Letters*. Edited by Rosamund Barlett, 111–112. Translated by Rosamund Barlett and Anthony Phillips. London: Penguin Books, 2004.

Chekhov, Anton. *Chekhov: The Four Major Plays: Seagull, Uncle Vanya, Three Sisters, Cherry Orchard*. Translated by Curt Columbus. Chicago, IL: Ivan R. Dee, 2005.

Clurman, Harold. *On Directing*. New York, NY: Macmillan Publishing, 1972.

Clurman, Harold. *The Fervent Years: The Story of the Group Theatre and the Thirties*. New York, NY: Knopf, 1945. Reprint: New York, NY, First Harvest, 1975.

Dean, Alexander and Lawrence Carra. *Fundamentals of Play Directing*. New York, NY: Holt, Rinhart, and Winston Inc., 1941.

Duke of Saxe-Meiningen, George II. Pictorial Motion. In *Directors on Directing*, edited by Toby Cole and Helen Krich-Chinoy, 81. New York, NY: Macmillan Publishing Company, 1953.

Edgar, David. *How Plays Work*. London: Nick Hern Books, 2009.

Foreman, Richard. *Unbalancing Acts*. New York, NY: Theatre Communications Group, 1992.

Fuchs, Elinor. "EF's Visit to a Small Planet: Some Questions to Ask a Play," *Theater 34*. 2004.

Fuegi, John. *Bertolt Brecht: Chaos According to Plan*. New York, NY: Cambridge University Press, 1987.

Goldhill, Simon. *How to Stage Greek Tragedy Today*. Chicago, IL: The University of Chicago Press, 2007.

Gorchakov, Nikolai. *The Vakhtangov School of Stage Art*. Translated by G. Ivanov-Mumjiev. Moscow: Foreign Languages Publishing House, 1960.

Graham, Scott and Steven Hogget. *The Frantic Assembly Book of Devising Theatre*. New York, NY: Routledge, 2009.

Grotowski, Jerzy, *Towards a Poor Theatre*. Edited by Eugenio Barba. Denmark: Odin Teatret, 1969. Reprint: New York, NY: Routledge, 2002.

Hansberry, Lorraine. *A Raisin in the Sun*. New York, NY: Vintage Books, 1994.

Hauser, Frank and Russell Reich. *Notes on Directing*. New York, NY: RCR Creative Press, 2003.

Johnston, Chloe and Coya Paz Brownrigg. *Ensemble-Made Chicago; A Guide to Devised Theater*. Chicago, IL: Northwestern University Press, 2019.

Jory, Jon. *Tips: Ideas for Directors*. Hanover, New Hampshire: Smith and Kraus, 2002.

Jory, Jon. *Tips: Ideas for Actors*. Hanover, New Hampshire: Smith and Kraus, 2000.

Kaufman, Moisés and Barbara Pitts McAdams. *Moment Work: Tectonic Theater Project's Process of Devising Theater*. New York, NY: Vintage Books, 2018.

Kiely, Damon. *How to Read a Play: Script Analysis for Directors*. New York, NY: Routledge, 2016.

Kiely, Damon. *How to Rehearse a Play: A Practical Guide for Directors*. New York, NY: Routledge, 2021.

Kirby, E. T. "The Origin of Nō Drama." *Educational Theatre Journal 25*, no. *3*, 1973, pp. 269–284.

Koller, Ann Marie. *The Theatre Duke: George II of Saxe-Meiningen and the German Stage*. Stanford: Stanford University Press, 1984.

Kulick, Brian. *The Elements of Theatrical Expression*. New York, NY: Routledge, 2020.

Loewith, Jason. *The Director's Voice, Twenty Interviews*, Vol. 2. New York, NY: Theatre Communications Group, 2012.

Mitchell, Katie. *The Director's Craft: A Handbook for the Theatre*. New York, NY: Routledge, 2009.

Nesmith, N. Graham. "Lloyd Richards: Reminiscence of a Theatre Life and Beyond," *African American Review, Fall*, 2005, Vol. *39*, No *3*, pp. 281–298.

Raymond, Caroline R. "Lloyd Richards: Reflections from the Playwrights' Champion: An Interview," *TDR, Summer*, 2003, Vol. *47*, No. *2*, pp. 9–33.

Rowell, Charles H. "I Just Want to Keep Telling Stories: An Interview with George C. Wolfe," *Callalo, Summer*, 1993, Vol. *16*, pp. 602–623.

Shurtleff, Michael. *Audition: Everything an Actor Needs to Know to Get the Part*. New York, NY: Bantam Books, 1978.

Sinek, Simon. *Start With Why*. New York, NY: Penguin Books, 2009.

Spolin, Viola. *Improvisation for the Theater: A Handbook of Teaching and Directing Techniques*. Chicago: Northwestern University Press, 1972.

Spolin, Viola. *Theater Games for Rehearsal: A Director's Handbook*. Chicago: Northwestern University Press, 1985.

Stanislavski, Konstantin. *An Actor's Work*. Translated and edited by Jean Benedetti. Oxon: Routledge, 2008.

Stanislavski, Konstantin. *My Life in Art*. Translated by Jean Benedetti. New York, NY: Routledge, 2008.

Toporkov, Vasili. *Stanislavski in Rehearsal*. Translated by Jean Benedetti. New York, NY: Routledge, 2004.

Tsubaki, Andrew T. "Zeami and the Transition of the Concept of Yūgen: A Note on Japanese Aesthetics," *The Journal of Aesthetics and Art Criticism* Vol. *30*, No. *1*, 1971, pp. 55–67.

Vakhtangov, Yevgeny. *The Vakhtangov Sourcebook*. Translated and edited by Andrei Malaev-Babel. New York, NY: Routledge, 2011.

INDEX